THE POLYMATH'S PATH

MASTERY BEYOND LIMITS

RUSHAN KHAN

Made with ♥ on the Notion Press Platform
www.notionpress.com

Contents

Contents

Acknowledgements

No mind is an island, and no path is walked alone.
If this book is a cathedral of multiplicity, it is built from countless stones, each quarried and shaped by those who walked with me, challenged me, and sometimes carried me when the path grew dark.

To my family—thank you for enduring a house of unfinished projects, late-night obsessions, and a mind always racing three steps ahead. Your patience and faith have been the quiet architecture beneath all my wanderings.

To my teachers, in classrooms and in life, who saw past my restlessness and nurtured my questions instead of silencing them. To the mentors who handed me forbidden books, who dared me to dissent, who welcomed my heresies as signs of life—you taught me that real knowledge is dangerous, and dangerously alive.

To my friends and kindred spirits at IIT Delhi, HRC, and far beyond: you are the parliament that kept my mind in motion. Each debate, every midnight brainstorm, every shared failure and unlikely victory—these are the true syllabi of a polymath's education. Thank you to the professors who saw rebellion as potential, and to the classmates who competed and collaborated with equal ferocity.

To my collaborators and colleagues—at Novasphere, Amazon, ISRO, and the United Nations—thank you for the privilege of building, breaking, and reimagining together. For every impossible deadline, every wild idea, every lesson learned in the field, I am grateful. You showed me that the boundaries between disciplines are illusions, and that the best work is always a conversation between worlds.

To the children I taught with the New Citizen Welfare Organisation: you reminded me that the greatest wisdom is often spoken with paint-smeared fingers, unpolished grammar, and eyes alight with curiosity. You are proof that the revolution begins wherever someone dares to ask "why" one more time.

To the researchers, artists, coders, linguists, and dreamers—known and unknown—whose work I have studied, borrowed, and stolen from, thank you for making the mosaic richer. Every citation, every margin note, every quiet act of genius has been a stepping stone on my path.

To my followers and community—on Instagram and beyond—your questions, challenges, encouragements, and even your doubts have made this journey less lonely, and infinitely more interesting. Your hunger for more is the kindling of this book.

And finally, to the reader.

Thank you for trusting me to walk with you through these twenty doors.

May you find, in these pages, not a finished map, but a mirror, a torch, and perhaps the courage to draw your own path through the wilderness of the possible.

— **Rushan Khan**

CHAPTER ONE

THE FIRST DEFIANCE — LIGHTING THE FIRE OF MULTIPLICITY

"The gods did not create one world, but many. The fool settles for the first; the wise set them ablaze."
— Attributed to Heraclitus of Ephesus, in the lost scrolls of paradox

I. The Birth of the Inner Rebel

There is a moment, rarely spoken of and even more rarely recognized, in the dim corridors of childhood when a spark flickers behind the eyes. It is not the spark of obedience, nor the gentle warmth of acceptance. It is the cold, blue flame of defiance—a question, primitive and electric, that ignites somewhere between the first "why" and the first "no.

"From the first day of schooling, the child is taught that the world is a machine of compartments. The bell rings, and the children shuffle, not just from room to room, but from self to self—mathematician at 9:00, artist at 10:00, silent observer by noon.

Curiosity is measured, rationed, contained. The fire is permitted only to warm, never to burn.

But the true polymath—though he does not yet know the word, though she cannot yet articulate the heresy—feels the choke of these invisible chains. The rules are suffocating, the walls too narrow for a soul designed to stretch, to sprawl, to consume the world in all its dazzling multiplicity.

This first defiance is rarely dramatic. It is not a shout, but a silent ache. A refusal to amputate parts of oneself for the comfort of others. A secret promise whispered into the dark:

I will not be less than I am. I will not choose one life when I feel the hunger for many burning in my marrow.

Every polymath is born twice: once into the world, and once into rebellion.

II. The Machinery of Conformity

Consider the architecture of modern society. Its institutions are factories, churning out specialists with the precision of clockwork. The educational system is the assembly line: each child a blank chassis, fitted with standardized parts, painted with the dull colors of practicality. The curriculum is a lattice of fences, each subject neatly partitioned, cross-pollination discouraged, curiosity punished with the red slash of error.

"Jack of all trades, master of none"—so goes the nursery rhyme of the conformists, whispered into the ears of the young like a hex. How cunning, how insidious, that the very phrase meant to warn against mediocrity is, in truth, a curse against greatness. They forget, or willfully ignore, the rest:

"But oftentimes better than master of one."

It is no accident. Specialization is not a law of nature, but a weapon of control. The specialist is predictable, safe, easily replaced. The polymath is a wild card, a disruptor, an irritant in the ointment of order. Society does not fear ignorance—it fears those who know too much, who cross boundaries, who see with many eyes.

The machinery of conformity is ancient and relentless. In ancient Athens, the polymathic Socrates was given hemlock; in Renaissance Italy, Da Vinci's notebooks were hidden away, his polymathy regarded with suspicion. In every era, the world has hunted those who refused to kneel at the altar of the One True Path.

III. The Hunger That Cannot Be Starved

Yet the fire persists. It flickers in the secret notebooks of the bored schoolchild, in the feverish scrawl of equations beside sketches, in the clandestine reading of banned books beneath moonlight. It is a hunger that outlives every attempt to starve it.

The polymath hungers for totality—a taste of every fruit from the garden of knowledge. Science and poetry, music and mechanics, philosophy and politics. The boundaries are illusions, lines drawn in sand by frightened men. The true mind is a tidal wave, erasing borders, flooding across disciplines with voracious joy.

Consider Hypatia of Alexandria, mathematician and mystic, who taught astronomy and philosophy with equal fervor, blending the sacred and the scientific in a single breath. Or Ibn Sina, physician and poet, who wrote treatises on medicine and metaphysics, refusing to sever the body from the soul.

What drives such minds? Not ambition alone. Not the lust for fame or the seduction of applause. It is something deeper, more primal: the need to see the world whole, to drink from every stream, to dance at every festival of the mind.

The polymath's hunger is not gluttony, but reverence. An act of worship.
To know the world in its fullness is to pay homage to the mystery of existence itself.

IV. The Fire and Its Dangers

But fire is not a gentle master. To light the fire of multiplicity is to invite danger, to play Prometheus and steal from the gods. The world will resist. The world will punish.

Isolation is inevitable. The polymath walks alone, misunderstood by specialists, resented by bureaucrats, envied by mediocrities. In a world of vertical ladders, the one who moves sideways is seen as a threat, a traitor to the creed of progress.

Worse than isolation is the constant risk of confusion, of being lost in the labyrinth of one's own making. The mind, stretched across too many fields, can shatter. The polymath must learn not only to gather, but to synthesize—to forge unity from chaos, to weave the strands into a living tapestry.

The world will call you dabbler, dilettante, fraud. You will be accused of lacking focus, of spreading yourself too thin, of knowing nothing deeply enough to matter. These are the weapons of the narrow-minded, the incantations of the fearful.

Yet every accusation is a signpost: you are threatening the order, violating the unspoken pact of mediocrity. The fire burns brightest when it is forbidden.

V. The Secret History of Defiance

Let us not be deceived: the history of civilization is the history of the heretic, the outlier, the rebel-mind. Every golden age, every renaissance, every convulsion of progress has emerged from the friction of multiplicity.

Archimedes, leaping naked from his bath, was not merely a mathematician but a poet of the possible, his curiosity ignited by every puzzle of nature. Nikola Tesla, a conjurer of lightning, dreamed in equations and hallucinations, fusing science and mysticism into a single vision.

Their stories are not anomalies; they are warnings. When multiplicity is denied, civilization stagnates. When it is unleashed, the world is remade.

The polymath is the secret architect of every revolution. The first defiance is the blueprint.

VI. Lighting the Fire: The Method and the Madness

How, then, does one light the fire of multiplicity? Not by mere accumulation of facts, not by the shallow skimming of a thousand surfaces. The true fire is lit by immersion, by the willingness to be consumed.

Begin with questions—the kind that unsettle, that refuse easy answers. Let them lead you across borders, into forbidden territories. Read outside your field. Listen to voices that contradict your own. Court confusion. Seek discomfort.

Abandon the need for approval. The polymath's path is littered with the bones of certainty. Embrace ambiguity, contradiction, paradox. Allow yourself to be remade by every discipline you encounter.

Synthesize. Do not merely collect—connect. Find the hidden harmonies between mathematics and music, between philosophy and engineering, between the art of war and the science of love. Every field is a lens; only together do they reveal the spectrum of truth.

Above all, protect the fire. Do not let it be snuffed by ridicule, by fatigue, by the slow poison of practicality. The world will try to tame you. Resist.

VII. The First Night: A Parable of Awakening

Imagine, if you will, a young woman named Elara, the daughter of a scholar and a seamstress, born in a village where each child must declare a single craft on the day of their twelfth year. The law is clear: the baker's son will bake, the blacksmith's daughter will forge, the scribe's child will write. Multiplicity is forbidden, under penalty of exile.

But Elara—strange, silent, unruly—cannot choose. By day she sketches birds in the dust, by night she eavesdrops on the astronomers in the hills. She learns to weave, to heal, to sing, to calculate the orbits of stars. Her curiosity is insatiable, her hunger incurable.

On the day of choosing, she stands before the council and refuses to speak. The crowd roars for punishment, but the oldest councilor, remembering her own childhood shame, intervenes.
"Let her be," the old woman says. "Some fires cannot be tamed."

Elara is shunned, but she persists. Years later, when a plague strikes the village, it is her knowledge—drawn from medicine, mathematics, music, and art—that saves them. The law is changed. The first defiance becomes the new tradition.

This, too, is the story of every polymath: exile, persistence, vindication.

VIII. The Sacred Act of Refusal

To refuse is not merely to break a rule; it is to declare oneself sovereign. The first defiance of the polymath is sacred, a ritual burning of the false idols of certainty and submission. It is a baptism in chaos and possibility. To say "no" to the world's categories is to say "yes" to one's own infinitude.

This refusal, when it comes, is quiet but seismic. It does not scream; it reverberates. The polymath, in their earliest moment of awakening, senses the hollowness in the demands to specialize. The world calls it rebellion, but for the polymath, it is necessity—a matter of survival of the soul. It is the refusal to let one's curiosity be amputated in exchange for comfort.

Outwardly, the world may not notice this silent revolution. Inwardly, everything changes. Every book becomes a potential portal. Every conversation a new corridor. The polymath's mind, newly released from its shackles, becomes a cathedral echoing with questions and obsessions, a forge where disparate ideas are melted down and alloyed.

IX. The War Against the Monolith

What is the monolith, if not the petrified corpse of the collective intellect—rigid, towering, casting a cold shadow over every green shoot of curiosity? The monolith is curriculum, dogma, tradition, the demand for obedience disguised as wisdom.

To defy the monolith is to risk being crushed beneath it. The polymath learns to fight in the shadows, to move sideways, to gather wisdom in forbidden libraries and unsanctioned dialogues. History's greatest minds have always been fugitives: Galileo peering through his telescope in secret, Ada Lovelace scribbling algorithms in the margins, Richard Feynman picking locks and safecracking the vaults of closed thought.

The act of multiplicity is subversive. Each new discipline taken up is an act of intellectual smuggling. Each synthesis is a jailbreak. The polymath does not merely rebel for the sake of rebellion; they rebel because the world as it is cannot contain the world as it could be.

The price of this war is often loneliness, exile, misunderstanding. But the reward is vision. The polymath sees further because they stand on a mountain of stolen treasures, assembled from the ruins of many empires.

X. The Anatomy of the Polymathic Mind

What is the mind of the polymath, if not a crucible for paradox and contradiction? It is not a library, but a living city—streets crisscrossing in impossible geometries, bazaars where merchants of mathematics haggle with poets and philosophers. Each new discipline is not a closed room but an open window, letting in the

But beware. The hunger for synthesis can turn to madness. The mind can become a labyrinth, tangled in its own associations. The synthesist must learn discipline: to prune the wild growths, to tend the garden of the mind, to separate genuine connection from feverish fantasy. Synthesis is a practice of both ecstasy and rigor.

VI. Parable: The Cosmic Weaver

Listen. In an ancient city, there lived a woman called the Cosmic Weaver. She was shunned by the scholars, who mocked her for collecting scraps—bits of lost language, feathers, stones, equations, maps, fragments of song. Night after night, she toiled in her attic, stitching her fragments together by candlelight.

One day, a scholar climbed to her attic and demanded to see her "useless collection." She unveiled a tapestry so vast that it spilled out the window and across the city. As the people gazed upon it, they saw their own lives—stories, sciences, loves and losses—woven together in a single cosmic design.

The fragments, meaningless in isolation, became a revelation in synthesis. The city, once divided by guild and class and faith, was united in awe. The Cosmic Weaver had not merely collected; she had conjured the cosmos.

VII. The Secret History of Synthesis

Civilization's greatest leaps have come not from those who mastered a single fragment, but from those who dared to gather and unite many.

- **Pythagoras,** who fused mathematics and mysticism, hearing the music of the spheres.
- **Ada Lovelace,** who combined poetic imagination with mechanical calculation to envision the first computer.

- **Santiago Ramón y Cajal**, the father of neuroscience, who drew neurons as if sketching a new universe.

Their legacy is not a series of isolated discoveries, but the birth of new disciplines—hybrids that reshaped what it meant to know, to create, to be human.

The history of progress is the history of synthesis: the crossing of boundaries, the marriage of opposites, the refusal to accept the world's fragments as final.

VIII. Synthesis as Rebellion

To synthesize is to rebel against the order of things. It is to say: the world is not complete, the map is not finished, the story is not over. The synthesist is a revolutionary, building bridges where others build walls.

Society will resist. The specialist will scorn. But the work is sacred. The fragments cry out to be reunited. The cosmos is not a puzzle to be solved, but a symphony to be played. Every act of synthesis is an act of creation—a spark that lights the darkness between the stars.

IX. The Infinite Horizon

The journey from fragments to cosmos is never finished. Each synthesis reveals new fragments, each pattern suggests deeper mysteries. The true polymath learns to dwell in this tension—incomplete, ever-becoming, always reaching for the infinite.

To synthesize is not to arrive, but to voyage. Each connection is a star in the night sky of the mind, each insight a new constellation. The cosmos is not a destination but a horizon—ever receding, forever beckoning. The journey is endless by design. And in this contradiction is invitation. The greatest minds in history were not those who banished paradox, but those who learned to dance with it. The world's deepest truths are not linear, but spiral; not solid, but shimmering.

II. Paradox as Fertile Ground

Paradox is not the enemy of reason, but its midwife. In science, the greatest discoveries begin as contradictions: the light that acts as both particle and wave, the cat that is alive and dead, the universe that is infinite yet born in a moment. In art, the tension between harmony and discord births the sublime. In philosophy, the contradiction between freedom and fate becomes the crucible of meaning.

The polymath's mind is uniquely attuned to the music of paradox. Where the specialist recoils, the polymath leans in, feeling the pulse of energy that comes from holding opposites together. It is in this generative tension—this refusal to resolve too quickly—that new worlds are born.

III. The Anatomy of Contradiction

Contradiction is not merely confusion; it is a structure, a pattern, a hidden order. The polymath recognizes that the world is not made of neat categories, but of overlapping, interpenetrating realities.

Consider the double helix of DNA: two strands, spiraled in opposition, holding the code of life. Consider the human psyche: longing for safety and for adventure, for solitude and for love. The deepest realities are not singular, but duplex—woven from threads that pull in different directions.

To embrace contradiction is to become supple, resilient, creative. The mind that can hold two truths at once without fleeing to certainty becomes a crucible for synthesis and transformation.

IV. Parable: The Two-Faced Sage

There is a story told among mystics of a sage who wore two masks. To the right, he spoke of order, discipline, and clarity. To the left, he whispered of chaos, passion, and doubt. His disciples quarreled. Some clung to the words of the right mask, others to the left. None could reconcile the two.

One night, a young disciple crept into the sage's chamber and found him removing both masks, revealing not a face, but a mirror. In the mirror, the disciple saw his own face, split by shadow and light.

The sage spoke:

"Do not fear contradiction. Fear only the refusal to see your own complexity."

V. The Historical Genius of Paradox

History's true giants were not those who solved paradoxes, but those who became them.

- **Leonardo da Vinci** was a scientist who painted, a painter who dissected, a pacifist who designed weapons, a dreamer obsessed with the mechanics of flight and the practicalities of war.
- **Simone Weil** hungered for both justice and annihilation, for solitude and solidarity, for God and for nothingness.
- **Niels Bohr** built a physics on the "complementarity" principle: light is wave and particle, not sequentially but simultaneously.

These are not flaws, but engines. Their contradictions were not weaknesses, but sources of endless invention. The polymath's secret is not to resolve paradox, but to become its living expression.

VI. The Polymath's Paradoxical Practices

How does one cultivate the art of contradiction? The polymath does not flee from paradox, nor does she cling to a single pole. Instead, she moves between them, letting tension become rhythm.

1. Hold Opposites Without Panic:
Let conflicting ideas coexist in your mind. Resist the urge to choose too soon. Dwell in ambiguity. Let discomfort be a sign of growth, not failure.

2. Seek the Creative Edge:
The richest insights come at the boundary between opposites. Stand where certainty dissolves into doubt, where order blurs into chaos. This edge is the birthplace of synthesis.

3. Ask Heretical Questions:
Dare to question your own certainties. What if the opposite of what I believe is also true? What if my enemy's worldview contains a shard of my own? What if every answer breeds a deeper question?

4. Practice the Double Gaze:
See every problem from at least two perspectives. The artist in you, the scientist in you, the philosopher in you—let them debate, contradict, intertwine. The polymath is a parliament of selves.

5. Embrace the Dance:
Contradiction is not a static dilemma but a dance. Move between poles. Sometimes you must be the builder, other times the destroyer; sometimes the skeptic, sometimes the believer. Let yourself be fluid.

VII. The Psychology of Paradox

To live with contradiction is to endure a special kind of tension. The specialist seeks relief in certainty; the polymath learns to metabolize anxiety into energy. This is not easy. The mind craves closure. But the polymath's genius is to resist closure, to stay unresolved, to let the mind remain open, porous, alive.

This tension is the seed of creativity. The most original ideas emerge from the collision of incompatible truths. The polymath's psyche is a crucible—volatile, pressured, alive with possibility. It is not a place of comfort, but of transformation.

Nietzsche wrote:

"You must have chaos within you to give birth to a dancing star."

The polymath's chaos is not disorder, but generative friction—a field where new possibilities spark into being.

VIII. Paradox and Power

Society fears contradiction because it cannot be controlled. The consistent man is predictable, manageable, safe. The paradoxical mind is a force of nature—unclassifiable, ungovernable, dangerous. This is why the polymath is sometimes shunned, sometimes revered, always misunderstood.

But paradox is a source of unmatched power. The one who can wield contradiction becomes a master of adaptation. While others freeze or fracture, the polymath pivots, improvises, reimagines. In a world that demands rigidity, to be fluid is to be unstoppable.

IX. Parable: The Sword-Dancer

In a distant land, a sword-dancer was famed for her impossible grace. "How can you be so swift and so precise?" asked her rivals. She replied, "Because I am never only one thing. I am both the sword and the wind; the edge and the dance; the threat and the invitation."

When her enemies came for her, she did not resist. She became mist, then thunder, then silence. In every contradiction, she found a new form.

X. The Infinite Dance

To be a polymath is to accept that you will never be finished, never resolved, never whole in the conventional sense. You are the dancer, forever moving between the poles of being. To stop is to calcify; to dance is to live.

The world will urge you to choose, to settle, to become one thing. Resist. Let contradiction be your element. Let paradox be your signature. The infinite dance is the ground of your power, the wellspring of your originality.

The polymath is not a puzzle to be solved but a riddle to be lived.

Law of the Polymath #5:

Embrace contradiction as your native tongue. Let paradox become your power, and dance on the edge where all worlds meet.

CHAPTER SIX

THE LIBRARY OF SHADOWS — WISDOM IN LOST AND FORBIDDEN KNOWLEDGE

"What is not taught is not always worthless. The greatest treasures are often buried in silence, waiting for the heretic's hand."
— Marginalia from a censored codex, anonymous

I. The Shadow on the Library Wall

Every civilization builds its grand libraries—cathedrals of knowledge, proud monuments to what is deemed worthy of preservation. Every civilization, too, casts shadows behind those shelves, where the forbidden, the forgotten, the dangerous, and the heretical are relegated to dust, fire, or oblivion. The polymath is drawn not only to the illuminated stacks but to these shadows, sensing instinctively that what is hidden or lost is often more vital than what is displayed.

As a child, the polymath feels the tug of the unspoken, the allure of the locked cabinet, the forbidden shelf. "Don't look there," the caretakers warn. "Don't read that." But the mind that hungers for totality cannot resist the gravity of the excluded. Every act of censorship is also an act of invitation, every bonfire of books a beacon to those who would know the world whole.

II. The Anatomy of Erasure

History is a palimpsest, written over, redacted, revised by those in power. The Library of Alexandria was not only a monument to what was known, but a graveyard for what could have been known. When the fires came, it was not only scrolls that were lost, but entire possible worlds—philosophies, sciences, heresies, dreams.

Consider the fate of Hypatia, philosopher and mathematician, whose teachings were erased by violence, her works surviving only in hostile quotations. Or the suppressed treatises of the Sufi mystics, burned for blurring boundaries between faiths. Or the lost music of ancient civilizations, silenced by conquest, preserved only in cryptic notations.

Every age has its Index of the Forbidden, its list of ideas too dangerous to survive. Today, it may be the quiet deletion of inconvenient data, the banishment of unfashionable theories, the ridicule of unorthodox thinkers. The shadow stretches long and dark across the centuries.

III. The Polymath's Heresy: Seeking the Unwritten

To be a polymath is to be a trespasser in the library of shadows. The true rebel is not content with the curated canon. She reads between the lines, listens for the footnotes, chases whispers in the margins. What others dismiss as obsolete or irrelevant, she treats as sacred. What was forbidden, she makes foundational.

The polymath knows that the gatekeepers—priests, professors, politicians—are not always guardians of truth, but often jailers of possibility. The heretic's mind is forged in the crucible of forbidden questions:

- What is missing from this story?
- Whose voice was silenced?
- What knowledge was erased to make room for the present order?

Every discovery is an act of resurrection. Every recovered text, a spark against the darkness.

IV. Parable: The Ink of Silence

In a forgotten city, a young seeker named Lira worked as an apprentice in the great library. Her duties were simple: dust the shelves, copy the classics, never question the catalog. But Lira was haunted by the gaps—the numbers that skipped, the titles torn from bindings, the empty shelves whose ghosts seemed to whisper at night.

One evening, she found a hidden door behind a tapestry. Inside was a chamber lined with black volumes—books written in a script no teacher had taught, filled with diagrams of impossible machines, poems to unnamed gods, treatises on sciences that did not exist.

She spent her nights deciphering the forbidden texts, learning their music. When the city's rulers discovered her, they threatened exile. But Lira had already become a stranger to their world—a citizen of the library of shadows. In time, outcast thinkers sought her wisdom, and her reputation spread like wildfire, fanned by the winds of forbidden knowledge.

V. The Architecture of the Shadow Library

What does the library of shadows contain?

- **The Pre-Scientific Sciences**: Alchemy, astrology, hermeticism—fields scorned by modernity but pregnant with metaphor, intuition, and the roots of new paradigms.
- **Suppressed Histories**: The stories of women, of the colonized, of the defeated; the wisdom traditions erased by empire and orthodoxy.
- **Anomalous Data**: Phenomena that do not fit, anomalies buried by consensus, black swans lurking at the edge of every discipline.
- **Occulted Techniques**: Forgotten crafts, mnemonic arts, arcane systems of memory, ancient meditations—tools for mind and spirit lost to industrial uniformity.
- **The Unfinished and the Untranslatable**: Projects abandoned at the edge of madness, books in languages no longer spoken, fragments awaiting the polymath's curiosity to bring them back to life.

Within these shadows, the polymath finds not only lost knowledge, but a freedom to think outside the cages of the present.

VI. The Shadow as Teacher

To embrace the library of shadows is to cultivate a stance of humility and boldness. Humility, because you realize how much has vanished, how fragile is the edifice of the "known." Boldness, because you must risk censure, ridicule, and even danger to recover what is buried.

The shadow teaches that knowledge is never complete, that every canon is provisional, that today's heresy may be tomorrow's gospel. The polymath learns the art of intellectual resurrection—piecing together truths from fragments, breathing life into what the world would rather forget.

More: the shadow is a laboratory for synthesis. In the chiaroscuro of lost and forbidden knowledge, strange hybrids emerge. The polymath dares to blend the rigor of science with the intuition of mysticism, the logic of mathematics with the lyricism of myth. In the shadow, new forms are born.

VII. The Psychology of Forbidden Knowledge

There is an allure to what is hidden, a magnetic pull toward the unsanctioned. The psychology of forbidden knowledge is as old as humanity itself. Adam and Eve, seduced by the fruit of the tree; Prometheus, defying the gods to steal fire; every child who reads by candlelight past curfew, every thinker who asks the forbidden question.

This desire is not mere rebellion. It is the engine of progress. What is forbidden is often what is feared, and what is feared is often what is most potent. The polymath's mind is not content with inherited boundaries; it seeks the edge, the outside, the unspoken.

But there is danger here. The pursuit of forbidden knowledge can lead to madness, isolation, or ruin. The polymath must learn discernment—to distinguish between the wisdom that liberates and the shadow that consumes.

VIII. The Return from the Shadows

The library of shadows is not a final refuge, but a crucible. The polymath enters to gather, to resurrect, to transform—and then must return, bringing the treasures of the forbidden back to the world of the living.

This return is perilous. The world may not welcome what you bring. The recovered wisdom may be met with scorn, censorship, or violence. But to hoard the shadows is to betray their gift. The true polymath is a bridge, a smuggler, a translator between worlds.

Each new insight, each forbidden fragment restored, becomes a seed of change:

- The occult becomes the foundation of a new science.
- The heresy becomes the gospel.
- The shadow becomes the dawn.

IX. Parable: The Night Scribe

It is told that there once was a night scribe who, forbidden by day to write his questions, spent each midnight penning them in invisible ink—questions about the stars, the soul, the fate of empires. Generations later, during a time of crisis, a child discovered the scribe's secret journal, its contents revealed by firelight. The city was saved, not by the wisdom of the canon, but by the courage of a question asked in the dark.

X. The Polymath's Shadow Work

To be a true polymath is to make shadow work your discipline:

- Seek what is hidden.
- Cherish the lost.
- Question the canon.
- Respect the forbidden, but do not be ruled by fear.

The world's progress is written not only in the authorized text, but in the palimpsest beneath, the erased, the overlooked, the condemned. The polymath's genius is to see that all knowledge is provisional, all canons incomplete, all wisdom shadowed by the unknown.

XI. The Infinite Catalogue

The library of shadows is infinite. Each forbidden question leads to another. Each recovered fragment reveals ten more. The polymath's journey is never finished. The shadows are not to be dispelled entirely, for they are the wellspring of wonder, the engine of renewal.

To live as a polymath is to stand forever at the threshold of the shadow library—one foot in the light of the known, one foot in the darkness of possibility, arms full of books the world has tried to forget.

Law of the Polymath #6:

Seek wisdom where others fear to look. Let the shadows be your teachers. In every forbidden fragment, find the key to a new world.

CHAPTER 7: INTELLECTUAL GUERRILLA — SUBVERTING THE TYRANNY OF SPECIALIZATION

"When the roads are watched, the wise travel by forest paths."
— Attributed to an anonymous samizdat, Eastern Bloc, 1976

I. The Fortress of Specialization

The modern world is built on castles of expertise. From the moment you enter school, you are funneled into tracks, labeled by aptitude and promise, and taught that the highest virtue is to become an expert. The specialist is crowned king, his domain carved with sharp borders and deep moats. Degrees, titles, and certifications become walls—impenetrable to outsiders, enforcing the illusion of mastery.

But every fortress breeds its own shadows. The walls that protect also imprison. The expert, so proud of his citadel, soon becomes a warden of his own mind—trapped by the very boundaries that define his power. The world outside the walls is left to the wanderers, the outsiders, the guerrillas. And it is here, in the wild places, that true innovation is born.

II. The Machinery of Division

Specialization, we are told, is the engine of progress. The assembly line, the silo, the research grant, the academic department—all are monuments to a doctrine that values depth at the expense of width. "Stay in your lane," the mantra repeats, "or risk being run over." The specialist becomes a cog in a machine too vast to see.

Yet, what is gained in efficiency is lost in vision. The machine does not dream; it only repeats. The specialist is rewarded for refinement, for incremental advance, for the perfection of a single instrument in a symphony he will never hear in full. Blindness becomes a badge of honor. The generalist, the boundary-crosser, is branded a dilettante—a threat to the order that keeps the wheels turning.

But history tells a different story. The greatest breakthroughs come not from the deepest tunnels, but from those who dared to tunnel sideways, breaking through walls, connecting what was never meant to meet.

III. The Polymath's Insurgency

The polymath is not a soldier in the armies of specialization. She is a guerrilla, moving through the forests between fields, refusing conscription into any single domain. Where the specialist hoards, the polymath poaches. Where the expert builds walls, the polymath digs tunnels, plants seeds, lights fires.

This is intellectual guerrilla warfare—subtle, decentralized, unpredictable. The polymath is a saboteur, disrupting consensus, questioning dogma, smuggling methods from one discipline to another. He is not interested in the incremental; he seeks the exponential, the catalytic, the explosive.

The world of the intellectual guerrilla is not mapped by syllabi or job titles. It is a landscape of connections, shortcuts, hidden trails. The polymath moves with stealth and agility, striking where the fortress is weakest—at the blind spot, the dogma, the unexamined axiom.

IV. Parable: The Weaver and the Gatekeepers

In the ancient city of Lydra, each guild kept its own gate. The masons mocked the tailors, the tailors the bakers, the bakers the healers. Guildmasters grew fat on their secrets, and apprentices spent lifetimes learning only a single thread.

One day, a young woman began to slip between the guilds, learning the language of stones, the rhythm of needles, the alchemy of bread, the pulse of the sick. She was called a trespasser, a thief. But when a great flood threatened the city, it was her synthesis—a bridge of woven stone and fabric, sealed with flour paste and herbs—that saved them.

The guildmasters, shamed, tried to erase her name from the records. But the people remembered the polymath, who walked the forest paths when the roads were closed.

V. The Tactics of the Intellectual Guerrilla

How does the polymath wage her insurgency? Not with brute force, but with cunning, with play, with relentless curiosity.

1. **Infiltration:**

   The polymath moves through disciplines as a spy, learning their codes, mimicking their rituals, reading their secret texts. She is fluent in many tongues, able to pass as native in any land.

2. **Sabotage:**

   Where the fortress is strongest, the polymath finds the cracks. He asks the heretical question, exposes the blind spot, introduces a foreign concept that destabilizes the status quo. The guerrilla's weapon is the unexpected analogy, the mischievous metaphor, the question no one else dares to ask.

3. **Smuggling:**

   The polymath is a smuggler of methods. She imports a mathematical technique into art, a poetic device into science, a biological principle into politics. The boundaries between fields become porous; secrets leak, ideas mutate, and new forms are born.

4. **Collaboration:**

   Guerrillas rarely fight alone. The polymath seeks allies—other wanderers, other rebels. Together, they form networks of resistance, circles of exchange, underground salons where forbidden ideas are cultivated.

5. **Disguise and Deception:**

   The intellectual guerrilla knows when to hide in plain sight. Sometimes, to survive, you must wear the mask of the specialist. But beneath the mask is the anarchic grin of the polymath, always ready to subvert from within.

VI. The Cost of Rebellion

To wage guerrilla war against specialization is to risk exile. The polymath is often misunderstood, labeled a dilettante, denied credentials, passed over for promotion. The specialist's fortress is defended by a bureaucracy of gatekeepers—editors, hiring committees, grant panels—all trained to spot and expel the heretic.

But the price of safety is sterility. The polymath accepts the cost of rebellion for the freedom to see, to synthesize, to create. While the specialist is praised in his own time, it is the intellectual guerrilla whose legacy endures. For every Da Vinci, there are a thousand forgotten guildmasters; for every Ada Lovelace, a thousand well-dressed clerks.

VII. The Historical Record of Insurgency

The annals of progress are written by guerrillas:

- **Benjamin Franklin**, who moved from printing to politics, from science to philosophy, always subverting, always connecting.
- **Katherine Johnson**, whose mathematical genius leapt the boundaries of race, gender, and discipline to put humanity on the moon.
- **Richard Feynman**, who delighted in breaking rules, picking locks, and explaining physics with the metaphors of a safecracker.

Their victories were not won by following the rules, but by inventing new games.

VIII. Parable: The Unseen Orchard

In a forgotten orchard, it was said that only the oldest tree bore fruit. The villagers, specialists in apple-picking, ignored the saplings and the wild brambles. One spring, a traveler arrived and grafted a branch from the wildest bush onto the oldest tree. The next year, fruits of a new color—and flavor—appeared.

The villagers declared it a miracle. The traveler called it a question: What else is possible when you refuse to harvest only from the expected tree?

IX. The Polymath's Code: Rules for the Guerrilla

1. Never accept the boundaries as given.
2. Question every axiom, especially your own.
3. Seek out the forbidden, the neglected, the trivialized.
4. Make connections where others see only walls.
5. Honor the specialist's depth, but never worship it.
6. Remember: The map is not the territory. The fortress is not the world.

To live as a guerrilla is to trust your own navigation, to value agility over security, to prefer the risk of exile to the safety of obedience.

X. Toward a New Ecology of Minds

Imagine a world not of fortresses, but of orchards—fields where knowledge grows wild, boundaries are porous, and every mind is free to wander. The polymath is not the enemy of expertise, but its liberator. In a true ecology of minds, the specialist and the generalist dance together, each nourishing the other.

The age of the fortress is ending. The age of the guerrilla is dawning. The future will belong not to those who guard the gates, but to those who invent the paths between them.

Law of the Polymath #7:

Wage guerrilla war on the tyranny of specialization. Move through the shadows, break the boundaries, and let no wall confine your curiosity.

48

CHAPTER EIGHT

THE HYDRA'S HEAD — MULTIPLYING SELVES, MULTIPLYING WORLDS

"To be many is not to be scattered—it is to be inexhaustible."
— Attributed to Heraclitus, from the lost fragments

I. The Myth of the Single Self

From the earliest days, the world whispers a lie: You are one thing. "Find yourself," they say, as if the self were a buried relic, singular and waiting to be unearthed. "Be true to yourself," as if truth were a monolith, not a shifting constellation. The myth of the single self is the myth of control, of predictability, of a life that can be mapped in one dimension.

But the polymath's spirit rebels. It senses multiplicity within, the presence of many voices, many hungers, many possible lives. The world calls this fragmentation, pathology, a weakness of will. The polymath knows it as abundance—a wellspring, a Hydra's head that, when cut, only grows more.

II. The Hydra: Monster and Metaphor

In myth, the Hydra is a beast of terror, a serpent with many heads. Cut off one, and two more emerge. Hercules, the hero of order, is sent to destroy it, for chaos cannot be tolerated. But what if the Hydra is not a monster, but a model? What if the multiplication of selves is not a curse, but a power?

The Hydra's truth is that life is not linear, nor is the mind. Each new head is a new perspective, a new faculty, a new world. The polymath's genius is to refuse the violence of reduction, to let the heads multiply, to see in the many the seed of the infinite.

III. The Architecture of Multiplicity

Within every polymath is a parliament of selves. The scientist and the artist, the strategist and the dreamer, the skeptic and the mystic—all jostle for voice and vision. The specialist is trained to banish all but one, to become a pure instrument. The polymath learns to conduct the full orchestra, to give each self its solo, its season, its secret hour.

This is not confusion, but orchestration. Multiplying selves is the secret architecture of creative genius. Consider Leonardo da Vinci, who wrote with one hand and painted with the other, who invented and dissected, who imagined flight and engineered death. Each discipline called forth a different Leonardo, each project a different man.

Virginia Woolf wrote of "a thousand shapes of thought." Emerson spoke of "a series of selves, each greater than the last." The polymath is not a single candle burning, but a constellation set ablaze.

IV. Parable: The City of Masks

In a city where each citizen wore a single mask for life, there lived a woman who changed hers each dawn. By day, she was a judge; by night, a dancer; by morning, a gardener; by twilight, a poet. The city's leaders called her faithless. "You cannot be trusted," they said. "You are not one of us."

But when crisis came—a fire, a famine, a plague—she became what was needed: healer, architect, singer of laments. The city survived, not by the constancy of its citizens, but by the inexhaustibility of the many-headed one.

V. Psychological Warfare: The Fear of the Many

Society is terrified of multiplicity. The specialist is predictable; the polymath is a shapeshifter, ungovernable, endlessly reborn. The world fears the one who cannot be pinned down, who slips between identities, who refuses to be summarized.

The fear is justified. Multiplicity is a threat to every system of hierarchy and control. The polymath cannot be managed, cannot be owned. Every time a new self is born, a new field unlocked, a new world discovered, the established order trembles.

And yet, the cost of denying multiplicity is spiritual suffocation. The single self is a coffin. The polymath's proliferation is not chaos, but survival—the only insurance against stagnation, despair, and the slow death of the soul.

VI. The Practices of Multiplying Selves

How does the polymath cultivate the Hydra's gift without becoming lost in her own labyrinth? The art is not one of endless division, but of creative multiplication and integration.

1. **Deliberate Role-Playing:**
   Adopt new identities as experiments. Write as a scientist, then as a poet, then as a skeptic, then as a mystic. Let each self speak without censorship. The friction between personas breeds insight.

2. **Boundary Dissolution:**
   Allow the edges between fields, roles, and selves to blur. Let your artistic failures inform your scientific hypotheses, your philosophical doubts shape your political strategies. Multiplicity is a web, not a box.

3. **Scheduled Polyphony:**
   Devote time to each self. The week is a stage for many actors. Rather than "balancing" life, orchestrate it—give each voice its hour, its project, its passion.

4. **Journaling the Parliament:**
   Keep a log of the voices within. Notice when the artist takes the pen from the engineer, when the strategist silences the dreamer. Learn who in you is neglected, who is overfed, who is dying to be born.

5. **Embracing Contradiction:**
   Let your selves disagree. The polymath's mind is a crucible for paradox, a meeting ground for conflicting desires. Do not force resolution; let the contradictions ferment into new questions.

VII. The Hydra in History and Legend

History is the record of those who multiplied themselves beyond recognition:

- **Benjamin Franklin**: Printer, inventor, diplomat, philosopher, scientist, statesman, wit—a new self for every crisis.
- **Rabindranath Tagore**: Poet, composer, painter, educator, reformer—each facet a gateway to a new India.
- **Sophie Germain**: Mathematician by night, philosopher by day, physicist in secret—a Hydra in a world that demanded she hide every head.

Their lives were not neat, not linear, not safe. But they were inexhaustible.

VIII. Parable: The Hydra's Garden

It is told that in a forgotten land, a gardener planted a single root. Each season, a new shoot emerged—one fragrant, one thorny, one bearing fruit, one blossoming only at night. The villagers begged the gardener to prune the plant, to force it into a single shape. She refused. In time, the garden became a living labyrinth, sheltering a thousand species, thriving where all others failed.

When drought came, the monocultures withered, but the Hydra's garden endured. Its multiplicity was its strength.

IX. The Polymath's Shadow: Risks of Multiplication

Multiplying selves is not without danger. The risk is diffusion—scattering energy, losing focus, becoming a ghost in one's own house. The polymath must learn not only to multiply, but to integrate, to weave the many selves into a resilient whole.

The shadow of the Hydra is madness—identity in fragments, never converging. The art is to let the heads grow, but to keep the heart united; to play many roles, but never lose the thread of becoming.

Integration does not mean reduction to one. It is the dance of many in concert, the polyphony of a mind unafraid of its own abundance.

X. The Infinite Worlds Within

The polymath's gift is to discover that each self unlocks a new world. The scientist's self reveals the world of law and pattern; the artist's self, the world of image and emotion; the philosopher's self, the world of meaning and doubt. Each world is a room in the palace of the mind, a window on the infinite.

The specialist lives in a single chamber. The polymath wanders the whole house, opening doors, rearranging furniture, inviting strangers to dine. The house expands with every new self. Infinity is not "out there"—it is within, multiplying as you dare to become more.

XI. The Law of the Hydra

To multiply selves is to multiply worlds. The polymath is not one, but many; not a straight line, but a branching river. The world will beg you to choose, to prune, to settle. Refuse. Become inexhaustible. Let your many heads grow wild, each one a gateway to a new cosmos.

Law of the Polymath #8:

Multiply your selves, and you will multiply your worlds. Let no one reduce you to one. In your inexhaustibility, become the infinite.

CHAPTER NINE

ECHOES OF DA VINCI — RECLAIMING THE RENAISSANCE SPIRIT

"He who knows most grieves most for wasted time."
— Leonardo da Vinci, Codex Atlanticus

I. The Lost Art of Wonder

There was once a time when to be learned was to be whole. When the boundaries between art and science, invention and intuition, craft and contemplation were porous as mist. The Renaissance was not merely an age—it was a vision, a fever-dream of human possibility. The polymath was not an anomaly, but the archetype: a soul ablaze with curiosity, chasing truth across every field, refusing to settle for one angle of the prism when the full spectrum beckoned.

Today, we invoke the Renaissance as nostalgia, a sepia-tinted fantasy. The world has grown suspicious of wonder, and the word "Renaissance" is used as a platitude, a marketing term, a hollow echo. The true spirit has been exiled to museums and textbooks, embalmed alongside the bones of old masters. Yet the need for its resurrection has never been more urgent.

The world is awash in information, yet starved of vision. We have technologies Da Vinci could never have imagined, but our souls are malnourished. We have experts in all things, and visionaries in none. We have lost the art of wonder.

II. Da Vinci's Unfinished Symphony

Leonardo da Vinci was not a man, but a movement—a living force field where disciplines collided and cross-pollinated. Anatomist, painter, engineer, botanist, cartographer, philosopher, heretic, dreamer. His notebooks are fevered cathedrals of curiosity, each page a battlefield where sketches, riddles, and calculations vie for space, where questions breed questions in an endless chain.

Da Vinci's genius was not superhuman intellect, but superhuman openness. He did not merely learn—he absorbed, dismantled, rebuilt. He saw the flight of birds and imagined machines; he dissected corpses and painted angels. He wrote:

"Study the science of art. Study the art of science. Develop your senses—especially learn how to see. Realize that everything connects to everything else."

His life was an unfinished symphony, a testament to the impossibility of total mastery and the glory of the quest.

III. The Renaissance as Rebellion

The Renaissance spirit was born in defiance. It was an uprising against the dogmas of church and guild, a refusal to accept inherited boundaries. The polymath was a subversive, a contrarian, a trespasser in forbidden libraries.

The Renaissance did not merely revive the classics; it shattered them and began again. In Florence, Venice, and Milan, the boundaries between painter and scientist, poet and architect, mathematician and musician dissolved. To create was to cross-pollinate, to steal fire from every altar. The Renaissance mind was a crucible, not a container.

Yet, the true inheritance of Da Vinci and his contemporaries was not technique but attitude—a ferocious hunger, a divine impatience, an unyielding faith that the world is knowable if only you dare to look at it from all sides.

IV. Parable: The Apprentice and the Spiral Stair

A young apprentice, eager to become a master painter, begged entry to Da Vinci's studio. "Teach me to draw," he pleaded. Leonardo handed him a dead bird and a clock. "Learn the bird's bones, and the clock's gears. Paint them both, then build me a machine that flies. When you have failed, come back and tell me what you learned."

The apprentice, bewildered, spent months in frustration. His drawings were clumsy, his machines collapsed. But in failure, he found a new seeing—the spiral of bone echoed in the spiral of the clock's spring, the rhythm of flight in the ticking of gears. When at last he returned, Da Vinci smiled.

"Now you are ready to learn."

V. The Death of the Polymath — and the Necessity of Resurrection

Why did the Renaissance spirit fade? The rise of bureaucracies, the professionalization of the academy, the cult of specialization—these are the tombs in which the polymath was buried. Knowledge became property, divided into fiefdoms. The university, once a playground for heretics, became a labyrinth of locked doors. The polymath became a curiosity, then a punchline, then a ghost.

But the world that killed the polymath is dying of its own narrowness. Crisis after crisis—climate, technology, politics, soul—erupts from the spaces between disciplines, from the blind spots of the specialist. The future will not be saved by single-track minds. Reclaiming the Renaissance spirit is not a luxury, it is a necessity.

VI. The Renaissance Practices for a New Age

How does one reclaim the Renaissance spirit in an age of fragmentation and overload? It requires deliberate rebellion and sacred play.

1. Radical Curiosity:
   Read far outside your lane. Learn new languages, both literal and symbolic. Seek out the lost arts: geometry, rhetoric, anatomy, harmony. Let every question breed ten more.
2. Embodied Learning:
   Draw what you study, build what you imagine, dance what you theorize. Knowledge is not an abstraction—it is muscle, movement, sensation. Da Vinci dissected bodies not just for science, but to paint truth into flesh.
3. Commonplace Books:
   Keep a living notebook—sketches, formulas, aphorisms, failed dreams. Let randomness reign. The Renaissance mind is a compost heap; genius blooms from unlikely juxtapositions.
4. Cross-Pollination:
   Invite other fields to dinner. Collaborate with the unlike-minded. Make your mind a crossroads—invite mathematicians to your poetry, engineers to your philosophy, artists to your algorithms.

5. The Discipline of Unfinished Work:

Resist the tyranny of completion. Da Vinci left thousands of unfinished projects. The Renaissance spirit is less about perfect products than perfecting the act of perpetual becoming.

VII. The Renaissance Mind in Exile

To reclaim the Renaissance spirit is to accept exile from the mainstream. The world will label you unfocused, impractical, undisciplined. You will be an outsider at every table and a heretic in every guild. But this exile is your birthright. The Renaissance mind belongs to no single tribe and serves no single master.

You will find your kin in the margins: in the hacker's den, the artist's garret, the garage laboratory, the midnight café. You will build new guilds, new salons, new secret societies. The age of lonely genius is ending; the new Renaissance will be a conspiracy of the curious.

VIII. Parable: The Garden of Infinite Paths

In the heart of a city that had forgotten its artists, an old woman tended a secret garden. Each path twisted and turned, leading to unexpected vistas—statues half-carved, fountains that sang in odd harmonies, sundials that kept time with the moon. Children stumbled into the garden and wandered for hours, emerging changed, their pockets full of seeds.

The city's rulers, suspicious, demanded to know the garden's plan. The woman laughed: "There is no map. Only curiosity leads you through." In time, the city's finest minds came to walk its paths, learning again how to be lost, and in being lost, to find themselves.

IX. The Echoes of Da Vinci

Da Vinci's notebooks echo still—across centuries, across disciplines, in every unfinished question, every forbidden experiment, every sketch that refuses to be categorized. His spirit is not a relic but a call to arms.

To reclaim the Renaissance is not to imitate the past, but to dare what Da Vinci dared: to become many, to see with all eyes, to touch the world with all hands. It is to accept that mastery is not a destination but a dance, that genius is not purity but wild, impure, restless connection.

X. The New Renaissance — A Manifesto

Let the world be awash in curiosity again. Let the boundaries between fields dissolve. Let every mind become a crossroads, every life a tapestry, every question a gate to a new domain. The new Renaissance will not be a return, but a leap—the birth of something unimagined.

The time is now. The world is ready for heretics, for crossers of thresholds, for children of Da Vinci who refuse the single track. Reclaim the Renaissance spirit. Refuse to be one thing. Become the garden, the unfinished symphony, the echo that refuses to fade.

Law of the Polymath #9:

Resurrect the Renaissance spirit: let curiosity be your rebellion, and unfinished questions your power. Become many, and echo through the ages.

CHAPTER TEN

THE SCHOLAR'S BLADE — SHARPENING CURIOSITY AGAINST CONVENTION

*"The sword unsheathed in the mind is sharper than any steel: it cuts
away the false from the possible."*
— From the journals of Ibn Khaldun

I. The Blunt Edge of Obedience

From the moment we enter the halls of learning, we are handed
dull instruments. Syllabi, rubrics, standardized tests—these are the
tools of convention, designed not to sharpen our minds but to
blunt them. The questions are safe, the answers predetermined.
The student's curiosity is not a blade but a kitchen utensil: useful,
predictable, incapable of drawing blood.

The world praises obedience in the guise of discipline. "Follow
the method," the teachers insist. "Trust the experts." The path is

well-lit, the boundaries clear. The price for stepping beyond them is ridicule, exile, or, worst of all, being ignored.

But the polymath refuses this bargain. The true scholar is a swordsman of the mind—restless, dangerous, unafraid to cut through the fabric of convention. Curiosity, honed and wielded as a blade, is the only weapon that can carve out new worlds from the stone of the given.

II. The Anatomy of Sharpness

Sharpness is not aggression; it is clarity. The dull mind accepts what it is given, mistaking repetition for understanding. The sharp mind interrogates every premise, questions every tradition, slices through jargon and dogma to expose what is living and what is dead.

Consider Galileo, who refused to accept the Ptolemaic sky. With telescopic curiosity, he cut through centuries of inherited "truth," revealing the moons of Jupiter and the phases of Venus. Or Hypatia, who sharpened her intellect against the dogmas of her age, paying with her life but leaving a legacy sharper than any blade.

The scholar's blade is forged in skepticism, tempered by humility, and wielded with imagination. Its edge is maintained not through memorization, but through relentless questioning.

III. Parable: The Blade and the Anvil

In a city ruled by tradition, a young scholar approached the blacksmith's forge. "Teach me to make a blade that does not dull," he begged. The blacksmith gave him a lump of iron and a question: "What is it you wish to cut?"

The scholar tried to forge a sword as he had been taught, but the blade bent and chipped. Frustrated, he returned. "You followed the recipe," the blacksmith said, "but you never asked why." The scholar began to experiment—adding carbon, quenching with oil, folding the metal, testing each flaw. Each failure was a new question, each question a whetstone.

In time, the scholar forged a blade that was sharper than tradition, sharper than fear—a blade that could cut through the very chains that bound his city.

IV. The Whetstone of Dissent

Curiosity is not sharpened in comfort. It is whetted against resistance. The scholar who never meets opposition becomes complacent, his questions soft, his answers flabby. The polymath seeks out the abrasive, the uncomfortable, the controversial. He courts dissent, knowing that only friction creates an edge.

This is the paradox of the scholar's blade: it grows sharper the more it is challenged. The mind that is never tested grows brittle and dull. The mind that is forced to defend, to re-examine, to revise becomes supple, resilient, lethal.

Consider the Socratic method—not a pedagogy, but a duel. The teacher wields questions like daggers, the student learns to parry with reason, to thrust with inquiry, to bleed for the truth. It is in this arena that the polymath is born.

V. The Rituals of Sharpening

How does the polymath hone curiosity against convention? Through a deliberate practice of intellectual swordplay:

1. **Challenge Every Dogma:**
   Ask, "Why must this be so?" Seek out the cracks in received wisdom. Every canon is provisional; every orthodoxy is a mask for someone's interest.
2. **Study the Heretics:**

Read the banned, the ridiculed, the forgotten. History's true advances began as heresies. The sharpest minds are those that cut across the grain.

3. **Debate Without Mercy:**

Engage with adversaries, not just allies. Seek out the strongest arguments against your own beliefs. Let your ideas be battered and reforged.

4. **Invent New Questions:**

Do not be satisfied with inherited puzzles. Forge your own. The world's greatest revolutions began with new kinds of questions.

5. **Practice Intellectual Swordsmanship:**

Learn from many masters—scientists, poets, philosophers, engineers. Each discipline is a different blade, a different technique. The polymath is a fencer with many styles.

VI. The Scholar's Solitude

To wield a sharp mind is to accept a certain solitude. Convention is a crowded room; the edge is a lonely place. The polymath walks often alone, misunderstood, feared, envied, sometimes betrayed.

But solitude is not isolation; it is the crucible in which sharpness is maintained. The scholar's blade is honed in silence, in reflection, in the secret duel with one's own ignorance. The world's noise is a grinding wheel—use it, but return always to the quiet where true sharpness is revealed.

VII. Parable: The Mirror of the Blade

It is said that the sharpest swords, when polished, become mirrors. The scholar's blade, too, reveals the face of its wielder. Every question you pose, every assumption you dissect, is a reflection of your own mind. The dull scholar sees only the surface; the sharp scholar sees himself, sees the world, sees the hidden seams.

In the end, the mind that dares to cut through convention discovers its own depths. The blade is not for destruction, but for revelation.

VIII. Against the Blunt World

The world will always seek to blunt your edge. Institutions reward compliance, not creativity; comfort, not courage. The price of sharpness is misunderstanding, resistance, sometimes exile. The polymath accepts this cost, knowing that a dull mind is a living death.

Sharpen your curiosity on the whetstone of every "no," every closed door, every rule that begs to be broken. Let your mind be dangerous—capable of cutting paths where none exist.

IX. The Scholar's Duel

The final test of the scholar's blade is not in the defeat of opponents, but in the creation of new worlds. The sharp mind is generative, not merely destructive. It slices through convention to reveal new possibilities, new forms of order, new kinds of beauty. The scholar's duel is with the future itself.

In the end, every act of creation is an act of incision—cutting away the false, the dead, the worn-out, to reveal what is living, possible, new.

Law of the Polymath #10:

Sharpen your curiosity against the stone of convention. Let your questions become your blade, and cut a path through the unbroken jungle of the known.

CHAPTER ELEVEN

THE ARCHITECT OF SYNTHESIS — BUILDING BRIDGES BETWEEN REALMS

"The river does not lament the distance between mountains, but rushes to unite them. So too the mind, when it is free, builds bridges from the disparate to the whole."
— From the meditations of Giambattista Vico

I. The Kingdoms Divided

The world is divided not by oceans or continents, but by invisible borders drawn through the mind. The academy, the marketplace, the laboratory, the studio—each builds its own citadel, policed by jargon and ritual, hostile to trespassers. The specialist reigns in his kingdom, master of a single dialect, deaf to the languages of neighboring lands.

These kingdoms are defended with the fervor of medieval lords. The artist scoffs at the mathematician's abstractions; the physicist dismisses the poet's visions; the philosopher is exiled to the margins, powerless in the court of policy. The polymath is the exile in all realms, never wholly at home, always searching for a path between.

Yet the most vital truths, the deepest powers, and the greatest acts of creation arise not within the walls, but in the no-man's-land between them. The world's progress depends on those rare architects who dare to bridge the chasms.

II. The Architect's Vocation

Synthesis is an act of rebellion. The architect of synthesis is not content to inherit the divided world; she sets out to unite it. Her mind is a blueprint, her curiosity the foundation, her creativity the mortar. She is not a tourist in foreign lands, but a builder, determined to make a home in the space between.

The true architect is not a collector of curiosities, but a weaver of structure—a designer of new forms that can bear the weight of difference. She does not merely borrow, but fuses. She does not merely compare, but transforms. Each bridge she builds is a new discipline, a fresh vantage, a pathway for others to follow.

The history of civilization is the history of synthesis. Every Renaissance is a bridge, every revolution a fusion, every leap in consciousness a collapse of borders.

III. Parable: The Bridge at Dawn

In a valley divided by a raging river, two villages lived in mutual suspicion. Each morning, the sun rose on their separate rituals, their children forbidden to cross the water. One day a child—curious, exiled, restless—began to gather stones, logs, ropes. For weeks, she worked alone at the river's edge, enduring mockery and doubt.

At last, as dawn broke, the first span of the bridge appeared, glistening with dew. The villagers watched, uncertain, as she crossed from one side to the other, bringing music from the west to the east, bread from the east to the west. In time, the bridge became a market, a meeting place, a new city born from the union of difference.

The architect of synthesis is this bridge-builder—unafraid to stand in the torrent, to risk the collapse, to invite the unknown with open arms.

IV. The Anatomy of a Bridge

What are the elements of true synthesis? The polymath-architect employs a secret grammar, a set of principles for uniting what others deem irreconcilable:

1. **Curiosity as Compass:**
   The architect begins not with certainty, but with wonder. She asks, "What if these two things, long separated, belonged together?" Her curiosity is ravenous, indiscriminate, hungry for the forbidden and the overlooked.
2. **Pattern Recognition:**
   The builder of bridges sees echoes and rhymes, analogies and symmetries. He is attuned to the pattern that repeats across domains: the spiral in a shell, the spiral in a galaxy, the spiral in a poem.
3. **Translation:**
   Synthesis demands fluency. The architect learns the languages of each domain, not to mimic, but to translate—rendering concepts in new forms, forging a shared vocabulary.
4. **Risking Collapse:**
   Every bridge is a wager. The architect risks failure, misunderstanding, even ridicule. Some bridges will fall. But

those that endure change the map forever.

5. **Hospitality to the Unfamiliar:**
   The architect does not demand that the foreign become familiar, but builds space for difference. The bridge is not a merger, but a meeting—a place where both sides retain their flavor but create something new together.

V. The Synthesis of Realms: Examples Across Time

The history of innovation is a ledger of bridges:

- **Leonardo da Vinci** fused anatomy and art, engineering and aesthetics, giving the world visions that still haunt our dreams.
- **Ada Lovelace** bridged poetry and mathematics, writing the world's first computer program as an act of imagination.
- **Santiago Ramón y Cajal** saw the nervous system as both forest and city, using the metaphors of architecture to map the mind.
- **Octavia Butler** crossed the worlds of science fiction and social prophecy, weaving new mythologies for the future.

Each became an architect of synthesis, each forged new realities from the tension between realms.

VI. The Tools of the Architect

To build bridges, the polymath must master certain tools—some ancient, some invented anew:

1. The Commonplace Book:
   A living record of insights, quotes, sketches, failures, dreams—a map of the mind's crossings.
2. Dialogue and Debate:

The architect invites others to the table—artists, scientists, mystics, skeptics—knowing that real synthesis is born in conversation, in the friction of disagreement.

3. Mental Models:

The builder constructs models that travel: metaphors, diagrams, equations, parables. These are the beams and arches of the intellectual bridge.

4. Prototyping:

Every bridge begins as a sketch, then a model, then a structure. The architect builds, tests, revises—accepting imperfection as the cost of innovation.

5. Resilience:

Not every synthesis will hold. The architect learns from collapse, gathering lessons to build the next, stronger span.

VII. Parable: The Weaver's Loom

A story is told of a weaver who sat between two rival villages, each famed for its distinct thread—one golden, one indigo. For years, neither would trade. The weaver, undeterred, learned the craft of both. She built a loom that could weave the two threads together, creating a fabric unlike anything seen before.

When famine struck, the villages found shelter together beneath her canopy. What was once a line of division became the place of gathering.

VIII. The Perils and Powers of the Bridge-Builder

The architect of synthesis is often misunderstood. The specialist sees her as a dabbler, the purist as a traitor, the bureaucrat as a threat. The bridges are sometimes burned by those who fear what they might allow to cross.

Yet, in every age, it is the bridge-builders who create the conditions for renaissance. They make possible the unforeseen, the hybrid, the monstrous and the miraculous. Their power is not in completion, but in connection. The polymath-architect's legacy is not a monument, but a network—a map of possible worlds.

IX. Rituals for the Modern Architect

If you would build bridges, practice these rites:

- Walk the boundaries.
  Visit domains not your own. Listen, observe, refuse the comfort of the familiar.
- Invite contradiction.
  Let opposing truths sit side by side. Synthesis begins in the tension between.
- Model relentlessly.
  Draw, diagram, story-tell. Make the abstract concrete, the distant near.
- Prototype failure.
  Build what does not yet exist. Let collapse teach you more than success.
- Gather fellow architects.
  Find other bridge-builders. Alone, you are a crossing; together, a new country.

X. The Infinite Bridge

There is no final bridge, no last synthesis. The work is endless—a perpetual reaching across, a ceaseless hunger to unite what has been divided. The polymath-architect lives at the edge, in the wind and water, moving always between, never content, never finished.

To be an architect of synthesis is to know that the greatest power is not in mastery, but in connection; not in the fortress, but in the bridge.

Law of the Polymath #11:

Become the architect of synthesis. Build bridges between realms, and let your mind be the crossing where new worlds meet.

CHAPTER TWELVE

THE DIVINE FOOL — SACRED PLAY AND THE POWER OF CHILDLIKE LEARNING

"To enter the kingdom of wisdom, become as a child: shameless, relentless, and delighted by the impossible."
— Attributed to the Gnostic Gospel of Sophia

I. The Exile of the Fool

Among all the archetypes the world fears, none is more dangerous than the fool. The jester, the trickster, the child—these are not the images of wisdom in a society obsessed with order, expertise, and restraint. Yet beneath the surface of every genius lies the soul of a divine fool, a spirit unbroken by convention, unafraid to ask the questions grown men deem unworthy.

The fool is exiled early. In the classroom, laughter is disciplined, wandering is punished, play is scheduled and sterilized. The world demands seriousness as the price of admission to adulthood. But seriousness, stripped of play, is only rigor mortis in disguise. The mind that cannot play is already dead.

The polymath knows this. She returns, again and again, to the fountain of sacred play—not as regression, but as resurrection. The fool is the secret king of learning. The world's progress depends on those who refuse to outgrow wonder.

II. The Child's Mind: Open, Unafraid, Insatiable

Observe the learning of a young child. Curiosity is not a duty but a reflex. Every object is a puzzle, every question a gateway. There is no shame in not knowing, no hesitation in asking, no hierarchy in what deserves attention. The child does not yet know the rules. Or, knowing them, delights in breaking them.

This is the divine state:

- To learn by touching, tasting, tumbling.
- To build castles of sand and reason both, and knock them down with equal joy.
- To ask "why" until the world frays at the edges, and then to ask "why" again.

The adult, in contrast, learns to hide ignorance. To ask only the safe questions. To fear the laughter of others, to dread the label of naïveté. The result is a calcified mind, brittle and anxious, terrified of appearing foolish.

The polymath's first rebellion is to reclaim the right to be a fool.

III. Parable: The Fool in the Labyrinth

1. In a city famed for its labyrinth, generations of scholars mapped every turn. The wise men warned, "Follow the prescribed path. The labyrinth is dangerous." But a young fool—laughing, singing, skipping—entered with no plan. He got lost, of course. He also found hidden gardens, secret doors, and a way out that no map had revealed.

The wise men called him lucky. The children knew better: He had played his way to freedom.

IV. Sacred Play: The Engine of Genius

Play is not mere leisure—it is the engine of invention. The greatest discoveries are born not from grim calculation, but from the joyful risk of trying the impossible.

- **Richard Feynman** fixed radios as a child, not by following manuals but by poking, prodding, and playing.
- **Nikola Tesla** daydreamed, building worlds in his mind before he built them in steel.
- **Mozart** composed as if at play, turning mistakes into music, improvising with the glee of a trickster.

The world's most profound advances begin as games. The divine fool is not content with the known rules; she invents new ones, breaks them, laughs, and begins again.

V. The Rituals of Childlike Learning

To reclaim the power of sacred play, the polymath practices deliberate rituals:

1. **Ask Forbidden Questions:**

Let no query be too simple, too silly, too obvious. The fool's question is often the lever that moves the world.

2. **Imitate and Transform:**

    Children learn by mimicry, but soon surpass their models. The polymath copies, then mutates, then invents anew. Imitation is the seed; play is the blossom.

3. **Experiment Without Goal:**

    Not all learning must be productive. The fool delights in process, not merely in result. Build for the joy of building, paint for the pleasure of color, code for the thrill of the unknown.

4. **Embrace Failure as Play:**

    The child does not mourn the fallen block tower. She laughs and builds again. The polymath, too, learns to treat failure as a game, an invitation to try differently.

5. **Turn the World Upside Down:**

    The fool is happiest when rules are reversed, hierarchies mocked, the impossible attempted. The greatest ideas come in moments of inversion, when the world is seen through the eyes of play.

VI. The Fool's Courage

Sacred play demands courage. The world despises the fool because he cannot be controlled. His laughter is a threat, his questions an affront to order. The adult who plays is feared, for she makes visible the arbitrariness of the structures others serve.

To be a fool is to risk humiliation, to endure misunderstanding, to wander in exile from the serious and the safe. But only the fool has the freedom to remake the world.

VII. Parable: The King's Riddle

A king, weary of his wise men's arguments, declared a riddle none could solve. Days passed in fruitless debate. A child, listening at the door, wandered in and laughed: "Why not turn it upside-down?" The answer was revealed, not by logic, but by play.

The king, chastened, made the child his advisor. The wise men grumbled, but the kingdom flourished. For in every crisis, the child's laughter opened doors no wisdom could unlock.

VIII. The Fool as Alchemist

The divine fool is the true alchemist—transmuting the lead of confusion into the gold of insight. Where the expert sees only a wall, the fool finds a window. The polymath's genius is not in knowing more, but in playing better:

- Combining the unrelated.
- Juxtaposing the absurd.
- Making the strange familiar, and the familiar strange.

The fool is a master of analogy, metaphor, and play. He is nimble where others are rigid, resilient where others break. The polymath's mind is a playground, not a prison.

IX. The Infinite Game

The greatest play is never finished. The divine fool knows that the world is an infinite game—one in which the goal is not to win, but to keep playing, to keep learning, to keep asking. Every answer is a new beginning, every failure a new game.

The polymath who embraces the power of the fool becomes inexhaustible. Every field is a playground, every problem a toy, every day a festival of possibility.

X. The Law of the Divine Fool

The world will tempt you to grow up, to become serious, to trade wonder for wisdom. Refuse. Let your mind be the kingdom of the divine fool. Play with ideas until they reveal their secrets. Laugh at the world's solemnities, and teach others to do the same. For all true learning begins in play, and all true mastery ends in wonder.

Law of the Polymath #12:

Let the fool within you lead. Play relentlessly, question shamelessly, and remake the world as your playground of discovery.

CHAPTER THIRTEEN

THE PHILOSOPHER'S STONE — UNITING ART, SCIENCE, AND PHILOSOPHY

"The philosopher's stone is not a secret substance, but a secret synthesis."
— Inscription from the tomb of Paracelsus

I. The Ancient Dream of Unity

Across centuries and civilizations, seekers have chased rumors of a miraculous object: the philosopher's stone. With it, alchemists believed, lead could become gold, sickness could be healed, mortality could be transcended. The stone was never merely a mineral—it was a metaphor for the ultimate synthesis. The dream was not only to change matter, but to reconcile opposites, to bridge the chasms between what the world insists must remain apart.

Today, the world is more divided than ever. Art is cordoned from science, philosophy exiled to abstract salons, each discipline defending its territory with suspicion. Yet the deepest thinkers—Da

Vinci, Goethe, Hildegard of Bingen—knew the secret: the greatest transformations occur when boundaries dissolve, when the stone is formed in the crucible of union.

The true philosopher's stone is not found, but forged—at the meeting of art, science, and philosophy.

II. The False Alchemy of Specialization

Modern alchemy is a parody of unity. The specialist is taught to perfect a single craft, to value precision over vision, measurement over meaning. The artist is warned against "muddying" her vision with logic or theory; the scientist is told to shun metaphor; the philosopher risks ridicule for straying into either's territory.

Yet, what emerges from these silos? Art, beautiful but mute; science, powerful but blind; philosophy, elegant but impotent. Each discipline, isolated, becomes sterile. The world is left with gold that cannot be spent, knowledge that cannot be lived, beauty that cannot heal.

The polymath refuses this false alchemy. She seeks the stone by uniting what has been divided.

III. The Three Faces of the Stone

1. **Art: The Language of Vision**

   Art is the oldest science, the first philosophy. Before the word, there was image; before the equation, the dance. The artist sees what is not yet, gives form to intuition, invents new senses. Art is the stone's dreaming face—the imagination that births all transformation.

2. **Science: The Discipline of Discovery**

   Science is the art of humility, the philosophy of doubt made method. It tests vision in the fire of experiment, turns wonder into knowledge. The scientist's gift is not certainty, but curiosity disciplined by rigor. Science is the stone's questioning face—the relentless pursuit that refuses to be satisfied with illusion.

3. **Philosophy: The Architecture of Meaning**

Philosophy gives structure to vision and discovery. It asks why, not just how or what. It is the mind's compass, refusing easy answers, demanding coherence, seeking the highest ground. Philosophy is the stone's reflective face—the wisdom that unites action and intention, fact and value.

The philosopher's stone is the fusion of these three. When art, science, and philosophy become one instrument, alchemy happens.

IV. Parable: The Stone and the River

In an ancient land, three travelers—an artist, a scientist, and a philosopher—came upon a river too wide to cross. The artist painted a vision of a bridge; the scientist measured, calculating the load and span; the philosopher pondered the meaning of crossing, the ethics of disturbing the flow.

Each alone was paralyzed. But together, they built a crossing: the artist inspiring, the scientist constructing, the philosopher guiding. The river was spanned, not by any one skill, but by the stone they forged in unity.

V. Renaissance Alchemy: Case Studies in Synthesis

- **Leonardo da Vinci**: His notebooks reveal not separation, but an incessant fusion—anatomy as art, engineering as poetry, flight as philosophy.
- **Goethe: Poet** and botanist, dramatist and color theorist, he revolutionized each field by refusing to choose.

- **Hildegard of Bingen**: Composer, healer, visionary, her music and medicine were inseparable from her mystical philosophy.
- **Santiago Ramón y Cajal**: His nervous system drawings are both scientific data and works of art, philosophy rendered in ink.

These are not exceptions, but blueprints. Their stone was not a relic, but a living method.

VI. The Rituals of Synthesis

To forge the philosopher's stone, the polymath adopts daily rituals:

1. Cross-Pollination:
   Read widely and promiscuously. Let art books inform your science, let philosophy reshape your painting, let mathematics inspire your poetry.
2. Embodied Experiment:
   Make learning physical. Build, draw, write, debate. The hands and senses are crucibles for ideas.
3. Dialogues Across Boundaries:
   Seek out collaborators who speak different languages—literally and metaphorically. The stone is forged in conversation, in translation, in the joyful friction of misunderstanding.
4. The Alchemy of Analogy:
   Use metaphor as a bridge. The greatest scientific breakthroughs began as poetic leaps; the most enduring art is saturated in philosophical insight.
5. The Ethics of Synthesis:
   Ask not only what is possible, but what is good and beautiful. Let every act of creation be guided by meaning as well as utility.

VII. The Philosopher's Stone and the Polymathic Life

The stone is not a single achievement, but a lifelong process—a practice of perpetual unification. Every new field entered is a new ingredient; every synthesis, a new alloy. The polymath lives at the crossroads, forging and reforging the stone in the heat of wonder, discipline, and reflection.

This is not the easy path. The world will mock your impurity, your wandering, your refusal to specialize. But the polymath is not deterred. She knows that to unite is to transform, to risk is to renew, to synthesize is to approach the miraculous.

VIII. Parable: The Alchemist's Circle

It is told that an alchemist drew a circle on the floor, standing at the point where all lines met. He invited artists, scientists, and philosophers to join him, each tracing their own arc. Where their lines overlapped, sparks leapt. There, in the center, the philosopher's stone emerged—not as a rock, but as a moment, a method, a marriage of minds.

IX. Toward the Living Stone

The future belongs to those who refuse to leave any part of themselves—or the world—outside the circle. The philosopher's stone is forged not by purity, but by union; not by certainty, but by wonder; not by mastery, but by the courage to mix, to meld, to risk imperfection for the sake of creation.

In a divided world, the greatest revolution is reunion. The polymath is the alchemist of the age, uniting art, science, and philosophy into the living stone that transforms all.

Law of the Polymath #13:

Forge the philosopher's stone within: unite art, science, and philosophy in every act. Let nothing remain divided that your mind can make whole.

CHAPTER FOURTEEN

THE CARTOGRAPHER OF THE UNKNOWN — MAPPING THE UNTHINKABLE

"The edges of the map are not warnings, but invitations."
— Marginalia from a lost chart of the Age of Discovery

I. The Tyranny of the Known

Society worships the comfort of the mapped. We are taught to cherish the well-explored, to recite what is known, to trust in the lines drawn by experts and elders. The world is divided into labeled zones—safe harbors, forbidden forests, the neat geometry of certainty.

"Here be dragons," the old maps warned.

But the polymath knows that dragons do not guard the end of the world—they guard its beginning.

The specialist lives within the boundaries of the known. The polymath is compelled to the edge, to the blank spaces, to the questions no one dares to write. For every map is a prison as much as it is a guide. The world's greatest treasures lie not in the center, but at the furthest edge—the place where the map dissolves into mystery.

II. The Ancient Art of Mapping the Unknown

The first maps were not tools of conquest, but confessions of awe. Early cartographers sketched the world as they imagined it: rivers flowing backward, monsters lurking, islands that shimmered and vanished at dawn. Each chart was a myth as much as a measurement, a story as much as a science.

But over centuries, the map became an instrument of control. The unknown was divided, conquered, "tamed" by the logic of empire and bureaucracy. The unthinkable was erased, replaced by the certitude of names and numbers.

Yet the mind of the polymath is undomesticated. She knows that every act of mapping is an act of creation—and that every unexplored space is an invitation to invent, to imagine, to become.

III. Parable: The Mapmaker's Mirror

In a forgotten city, a mapmaker was famed for her accuracy. Yet her walls were lined with blank parchment. When asked why, she replied: "A true map is more mirror than portrait. It shows not only where we have been, but where we have yet to dream."

Each night, she listened to rumors: lost cities, invisible mountains, rivers that ran beneath the earth. She sketched what others refused to believe. In time, explorers returned with tales that matched her impossible maps. The world's borders shifted, and the city thrived on the riches found beyond its certainties.

IV. The Polymath's Compass: Navigating the Unthinkable

How does one map what has never been mapped? The polymath develops a unique set of tools and rituals, a cartography of the possible:

1. **Cultivate the Art of Not-Knowing:**
   The beginner's mind is the true compass. The polymath admits ignorance, asks what others ignore, and allows confusion to become a guide.
2. **Follow the Anomalies:**
   The edge of the map is marked not just by blankness, but by anomalies—outliers, paradoxes, exceptions. These are not errors to be erased, but portals to the new.
3. **Draw Provisional Maps:**
   The first chart is always wrong. The polymath sketches, erases, redraws—knowing that every outline is a hypothesis, every border a bet.
4. **Blend Myth with Measurement:**
   The world's great discoveries are born from the union of dream and discipline. The cartographer of the unknown listens to legends as closely as to data, letting the improbable inform the possible.
5. **Invite Other Cartographers:**
   Mapping the unthinkable is a collective act. The polymath seeks out other explorers—artists, hackers, mystics, contrarians—each with their own compass, their own star.

V. The Maps of Imagination

All innovation begins as a sketch on the edge of the impossible.

- **Copernicus** drew a solar system no one could see.
- **Ada Lovelace** mapped a future of thinking machines.
- **Carl Jung** charted the unconscious, giving form to the formless.

These were not mere dreams—they were invitations for others to venture further. Every great leap is preceded by a map that dares to draw what does not yet exist.

The polymath's imagination is not an escape from reality, but a tool for its expansion. To imagine the unthinkable is to make it possible.

VI. The Courage to Get Lost

Mapping the unknown is an act of radical courage. The polymath must be willing to get lost, to wander in uncertainty, to risk ridicule and failure. The safe traveler never discovers new worlds.

The greatest explorers were not the bravest sailors, but the boldest questioners—the ones who asked, "What if the map is wrong? What if the world is wider, deeper, stranger than we can fathom?"

To get lost is to be found anew.

VII. Parable: The Cartographer's Child

A child, forbidden to leave the city walls, drew maps of imaginary lands. One day, a plague forced the citizens to flee. The only guide was the child's map, drawn from dreams. It led them through forests, across rivers, to a hidden valley the elders had forgotten. The city was reborn, not by the wisdom of the old, but by the vision of the untraveled.

VIII. The Ethics of New Mapping

With every new map comes responsibility. The power to name and describe is the power to shape reality. The cartographer of the unknown is not a conqueror, but a steward. She does not erase what is already there; she adds layers, reveals connections, honors the indigenous, the invisible, the lost.

Mapping is an act of humility as much as ambition. The polymath asks not only, "What can I chart?" but "Who is missing from this map?" The future belongs to those who draw with compassion as well as imagination.

IX. The Infinite Frontier

There will always be new edges. The world expands as we dare to imagine it. The polymath's work is never finished. Every map, no matter how complete, is a prelude to a new journey—a question folded into a promise.

The cartographer of the unknown learns to love the unfinished, the uncertain, the shimmering horizon. She lives at the frontier, one foot in what is, one foot in what might be.

X. Law of the Cartographer

The specialist perfects the known; the polymath invents the possible. The map is never the territory. The world is unfinished, and so must be your vision of it. Draw beyond the lines. Chart what others dare not. Become the cartographer of the unthinkable.

Law of the Polymath #14:

Map the unknown. Let your curiosity redraw the world. Where others see the end of the map, begin your journey.

CHAPTER FIFTEEN

THE ORDEAL OF SOLITUDE — MASTERING ISOLATION AND INNER DIALOGUE

"The one who fears being alone is condemned to echo the crowd. Solitude is the crucible where the self is forged, and the many selves are made to converse."
— Marginalia, found in the cell of a forgotten mystic

I. The Exile's Threshold

The path of the polymath is, inescapably, a lonely road. To embrace multiplicity is to risk exile from the warm herd of the specialists, to be misunderstood by those who worship the comfort of consensus. The rebel mind, by its nature, is cast out—sometimes gently, often violently. The price of difference is distance.

Society is structured against solitude. From birth, we are surrounded by noise: lessons, lectures, media, the ceaseless hum of the collective. We are taught to fear the silence where the voice of the self can be heard. The specialist finds safety in the company of peers; the polymath, if she is honest, must grow accustomed to the cold air at the edge of things.

Yet, solitude is not a punishment but a passage. The ordeal of isolation is the rite through which the polymath is reborn—not as a single self, but as a parliament of inner voices. The exile's threshold is the gate to mastery.

II. The Myths and Terrors of Isolation

The world paints solitude as deprivation, as a wound. The solitary are suspect: hermits, madmen, outcasts. It is whispered that isolation breeds arrogance, delusion, even madness. There is truth in these fears. The mind, left unchecked, can spiral—into paranoia, despair, or narcissism.

But there is another tradition, older and deeper: the mystics, the sages, the inventors, and the poets who have sought out solitude as a furnace of creation. Pythagoras in his cave, Hypatia in her study, Newton under the apple tree, Beethoven in his silent rooms. Their solitude was not emptiness, but fullness—a retreat into the interior wilderness where new worlds are born.

The ordeal is real. To master solitude is to master the self, to transform loneliness into generative aloneness, and to learn the rare art of inner dialogue.

III. Parable: The Watcher at the Window

In a city famed for its festivals, there lived a young woman who refused every invitation. She was called proud, then strange, then forgotten. Night after night, she sat by her window, watching the stars and listening to her thoughts.

Years passed. One day, a drought struck the city. The festival-goers, frantic for distraction, came to her door. She led them into her garden, which she had cultivated in silence—herbs, fruit, water from a hidden well. In her solitude, she had learned the secret rhythms of the earth. The city was saved by what she had grown in her time alone.

IV. The Practice of Inner Dialogue

The polymath's solitude is not a barren silence, but a theater of voices. The mind becomes an agora, a debating chamber, a confessional. To master isolation is to learn to converse with one's many selves—skeptic and dreamer, scientist and artist, child and sage.

1. **Cultivate the Witness:**
   The first voice is that of the witness: the part of the mind that observes without judgment. In solitude, the witness rises—a calm presence that listens to all others, that can endure discomfort and ambiguity.
2. **Summon the Council:**
   The polymath does not suppress contradiction but invites it. Let all your selves speak. Write dialogues between your personas. Allow the artist to challenge the engineer, the poet to interrogate the philosopher. In this council, synthesis is born.
3. **Practice Radical Honesty:**
   Solitude strips away the masks we wear for others. In isolation, self-deception becomes harder to maintain. The ordeal of solitude is the ordeal of truth. The polymath learns to face her ignorance, her fears, her contradictions—and to turn them to fuel.
4. **Invent and Rehearse:**
   Use solitude to rehearse new selves, to try on new voices, to practice skills and arguments without fear of ridicule. The mind

in isolation is a laboratory, a rehearsal stage, a forge.

5. **Listen for the Unheard:**

In silence, the whispers of intuition grow louder. The polymath learns to hear the subtle signals that are drowned out by noise—the hunch, the image, the fragment of a dream. Solitude is the tuning fork of genius.

V. The Gifts of Solitude

The ordeal of solitude, endured and mastered, bestows rare gifts:

- Clarity:
Away from distraction and demand, the mind sees more deeply into itself and the world. Insights emerge unbidden, patterns coalesce, connections spark.
- Resilience:
The polymath, forged in solitude, becomes less dependent on external validation. She grows self-sustaining, able to withstand ridicule, neglect, and the loneliness of the long journey.
- Originality:
Only in solitude can the truly new emerge. The mind, unshackled from consensus, can invent, imagine, and create without fear of censure.
- Empathy:
Paradoxically, the one who has walked the deserts of isolation is more able to meet others in their own exile. The polymath returns from solitude not as a recluse, but as a bridge.

VI. Parable: The Hermit's Mirror

It is said that a hermit, living alone in the wilderness, polished a mirror for years until it showed not only his own face, but the faces of all who came to visit. In his solitude, he had discovered the common root beneath every difference. The mirror, carried back to the city, became a sacred object—proof that the deepest solitude is the source of the deepest connection.

VII. The Dangers: Madness and Stagnation

Not all who wander alone return whole. Solitude can curdle into bitterness, or slide into despair. The polymath must be vigilant. Too much isolation breeds solipsism, obsession, the echo chamber of the self. The ordeal is to remain open—to seek dialogue within, but also to return, again and again, to the world of others.

The mind left utterly alone can become monstrous. The trick is movement: into solitude, and back out; into dialogue, and back into silence. The dance between the two is the heart of polymathic mastery.

VIII. Rituals of the Solitary Mind

To master the ordeal of solitude, the polymath develops rituals:

- Daily Retreat:
  Carve out time each day for silence and reflection. Guard it fiercely.
- Journaling and Dialogue:
  Write letters to yourself, stage arguments between your inner voices. Make the mind visible.
- Walks in Nature:
  Solitude does not require confinement. Wander in wild places. Let the mind expand into landscape.
- Meditation and Contemplation:

Sit with discomfort. Let thoughts come and go without judgment. The mind will reveal its treasures in time.

- Purposeful Return:

After solitude, seek out the company of others. Share what you have found. The ordeal is only complete when the gifts of isolation are offered back to the world.

IX. The Return from Exile

The final act of the solitary ordeal is the return. The polymath, remade in isolation, re-enters society as a stranger and a gift-bearer. She brings new insights, new syntheses, new ways of seeing. Her solitude was not an escape, but a journey to the source—a wellspring from which the world may drink.

The crowd will not always understand. Some will fear the one who has walked alone. But the world is remade by the gifts of the exile, the speech of the silent, the bridges built in solitude.

X. The Law of Solitude

Solitude is not a curse, but a crucible. Master it, and you master the parliament of selves. Endure the ordeal, and you will return with treasures no crowd can imagine.

Law of the Polymath #15:

Let solitude be your forge. In the silence, convene your inner council, and return to the world bearing the gifts found only in exile.

CHAPTER SIXTEEN

MASKS OF THE POLYMATH — IDENTITY, PERFORMANCE, AND INTELLECTUAL ESPIONAGE

"The world worships the single face, but the gods delight in the masked."
— Inscription on a Venetian carnival mask, 1512

I. The Tyranny of the Consistent Self

Modernity is obsessed with authenticity. We are told to "find ourselves," to "be true," as if identity were a buried coin or a fixed essence. Each resume, each passport, each social profile asks: "Who are you?"—and demands a single, marketable answer. The world rewards those who can be summarized, explained, classified.

But the polymath is a subversive to this cult of consistency. To be many is to be suspect. The specialist is pure, the polymath impure—unfixed, unpredictable, ungovernable. The age fears the mask, for the mask reveals the great lie: that identity is not a monument, but a stage; not a substance, but a performance.

II. *The Theatre of Knowledge*

All learning is theatre. The child plays at being scientist, artist, explorer; the adult is told to choose one costume and never remove it. But the polymath refuses the script. She changes costumes at will—sometimes out of curiosity, sometimes from necessity, sometimes for sheer mischief.

To perform many selves is not to be false, but to be fertile. Every new mask brings a new vantage, a new set of tools, a new set of permissions. The polymath knows that the self is not a prison, but a wardrobe. To live fully is to act, to improvise, to infiltrate.

Consider Leonardo da Vinci, whose notebooks are a masquerade of identities—engineer, anatomist, painter, poet, cryptographer, clown. Or Maya Angelou, who was dancer, journalist, activist, singer, memoirist, and more. Their genius was their refusal to be only one thing.

III. *Parable: The Festival of a Thousand Faces*

In the city of Miraggio, once a year, all citizens donned masks and swapped professions. The baker became a judge; the judge, a gardener; the child, a mayor. For one day, the city thrived in joyful chaos. The next day, the masks came off, and the old order returned. But the wisest citizens remembered the feeling of those borrowed faces—the new skills, the secret strengths, the freedom of performance.

The polymath lives every day as if the festival never ended.

IV. The Mask as Tool and Weapon

Masks are not just disguises; they are tools for survival in a world ruled by gatekeepers. The polymath learns to blend in, to speak the shibboleths, to pass among the specialists without raising alarms. This is not deceit, but strategy—intellectual espionage in hostile territory.

1. **Adaptive Camouflage:**
   In some domains, the polymath must wear a mask to gain entry: the lab coat in the laboratory, the suit in the boardroom, the jargon of the tribe. This is the art of passing—of knowing what to show and what to hide.
2. **Espionage and Extraction:**
   Once inside, the polymath gathers secrets, methods, contacts, and knowledge. He notes the blind spots, the rituals, the unspoken taboos. Then, just as quietly, he disappears—taking the treasure to new lands, cross-pollinating, destabilizing.
3. **Performance as Resistance:**
   The mask is also a shield. When the world demands confession, the polymath performs ambiguity. When the authorities demand allegiance, the polymath answers with riddles, with satire, with the sly smile of the trickster.

V. The Dangers of Disguise

To wear many masks is also to risk becoming lost. The polymath may forget his own face, may drift into imposture or duplicity. There is a shadow side to performance: the temptation to manipulate, to deceive, to become hollow.

The answer is not to strip away all masks, but to learn to return home. The wise polymath maintains a sanctuary—a private space where no performance is required, where the inner council can meet without pretense. The mask is a tool, not a master.

VI. Historical Espionage: The Polymath as Spy

History's greatest minds were often spies—not only in war, but in culture, in thought.

- **Benjamin Franklin** slipped between countries, professions, and allegiances, gathering intelligence for revolution.
- **T.E. Lawrence** moved between tribes, nations, and mythologies, performing a dozen selves for a dozen causes.
- **Sophie Germain** posed as "Monsieur LeBlanc" to infiltrate the mathematical societies that barred women from entry.

Their mastery was not only of knowledge, but of navigation—of knowing when to hide, when to reveal, when to vanish.

VII. The Rituals of Multiplicity

To thrive amid masks, the polymath develops rituals:

1. **Conscious Shapeshifting:**
   Practice becoming someone else—adopt the language, the posture, the mindset of a new field. Learn to move between registers without friction.
2. **Journaling the Selves:**
   Keep a record of your performances. Which masks empower you? Which drain you? Which open doors, and which close them?
3. **Strategic Vulnerability:**

Occasionally, let the mask slip. Show a hint of the true council within. This builds trust, forges alliances, and reminds the world that multiplicity is a form of honesty.

4. **The Return to Center:**
   After each performance, retreat to solitude. Review what was learned, what was lost, what new face wishes to be born.

VIII. Parable: The Maskmaker's Apprentice

A maskmaker taught her apprentice to carve a hundred faces—joy, rage, sorrow, serenity. The apprentice asked, "Which is the real one?" The maskmaker replied, "The one you wear when you are alone, dreaming up the next."

IX. The Law of the Mask

The world will always demand your true face. The polymath answers by wearing a thousand. Identity is not a confession, but a choreography; not a secret to be uncovered, but a garden to be cultivated. Only those who master the dance of masks can move freely through all domains.

Law of the Polymath #16:

Master the art of the mask. Let identity be your instrument, performance your strategy, and movement between worlds your secret power.

CHAPTER SEVENTEEN

THE DANCE OF TIME — CHRONOMASTERY AND THE ECONOMICS OF ATTENTION

"You may possess many worlds, but only one hour at a time."
— From the journals of Seneca, written on the edge of exile

I. The Tyranny and Illusion of Time

Time is the only truly universal currency. The specialist, the polymath, the fool, and the king each wake to the same twenty-four hours. Yet modernity's myth is that time can be hoarded, stretched, or conquered with sufficient discipline and technology. We are told we can "manage" it, as if time were a servant and not a sovereign.

But the polymath soon discovers the lie: time is not managed, it is danced with. Every act of creation is a negotiation with the hourglass, every act of attention a wager against entropy. The polymath's life is a labyrinth of pursuits, each demanding its own season, its own tempo, its own cost.

Society, obsessed with productivity, worships the schedule. The calendar becomes a cage, the to-do list a confession of finitude. Yet true mastery of time—chronomastery—demands a subtler art: to know not only how to spend time, but how to let it spend you.

II. The Economy of Attention

If time is currency, attention is its coin. The modern world is an endless marketplace, each vendor clamoring for your gaze. Notifications, deadlines, the ceaseless scroll—an architecture of distraction designed to keep you in perpetual transaction.

The specialist is taught to focus, to narrow the spotlight, to shun all but the sanctioned task. The polymath, by contrast, courts breadth and depth both—juggling multiple fields, projects, obsessions. The risk is diffusion, the shadow of the dabbling dilettante. But the true polymath learns to invest attention, not scatter it.

Chronomastery is not ruthless exclusion; it is deliberate orchestration. Each field, each project, is a dancer in the troupe. The choreographer is attention itself, knowing when to give the solo, when to blend the chorus, when to call for silence.

III. Parable: The Clockmaker's Paradox

In a village famed for its timepieces, a clockmaker built a clock that could strike every hour at once. The townsfolk marveled, but soon grew anxious—life became a cacophony, every moment indistinguishable from the next. The clockmaker dismantled his masterpiece and built a sundial instead, one that cast a single, clear shadow.

The lesson: to mark time is to choose. To live is to say yes to some hours, and no to others.

IV. The Polymath's Dance Steps: Rituals of Chronomastery

How does the polymath master time without becoming its slave?

1. **Seasons of Focus:**

   The mind, like the earth, has seasons. There are months for science, weeks for poetry, days for wandering. The polymath learns to rotate crops, to let fields lie fallow, to trust in cycles rather than rigid routines.

2. **Monastic Intervals:**

   Solitude is the crucible of depth. The polymath carves out "cells" of uninterrupted time—hours or days devoted to a single pursuit. Within these walls, distraction dies and work becomes prayer.

3. **Deliberate Polyphony:**

   The schedule is not a list but a score. Projects are voices in a fugue, each entering and receding. The polymath practices polyphonic living, letting themes echo and intertwine, never mistaking noise for music.

4. **Sabbaths of Silence:**

   To do nothing is to reclaim the hour. The polymath honors the day of rest, the time for idleness, the sacred pause. In silence, the mind digests, integrates, renews.

5. **Mindful Expenditure:**

   Attention is not infinite. The polymath learns to spend it as a miser spends gold—lavishly on what matters, frugally on what does not. The price of mastery is the courage to ignore.

V. The Shadow of Multiplicity: The Cost of the Dance

To be many is to risk dissipation. The polymath is haunted by the specter of wasted time, of unfinished projects, of genius dispersed too thin. The world will accuse: "Jack of all trades, master of none." The calendar fills with ghosts—abandoned ambitions, lost years.

But this is the necessary risk of the dance. The polymath accepts the cost, knowing that a life spent in a single room is no life at all. The goal is not to finish every song, but to have danced to many.

VI. The Economics of Saying No

Every "yes" is a "no" to a thousand possible worlds. The polymath's art is not only in choosing, but in refusing. The power to say no—to distraction, to obligation, to the tyranny of the urgent—is the only way to preserve the space for the essential, the wild, the truly interesting.

The specialist says no to all but one thing. The polymath says yes to much, but must become ruthless in pruning the trivial many in favor of the vital few. The greatest works are born from the courage to neglect what is merely urgent in order to nourish what is truly important.

VII. Parable: The Weaver of Days

A weaver, given a single skein of golden thread, could have made a perfect scarf. Instead, she unraveled the thread and wove it into a vast tapestry, flawed but magnificent—scenes of every season, every joy, every sorrow. The scarf would have been finished; the tapestry was never done. Yet it warmed generations.

So with the polymath: the days may be unfinished, but the pattern endures.

VIII. The New Calendar: Designing a Polymathic Life

To master the dance of time, the polymath must create a new calendar—not a grid of hours to be filled, but a living architecture of purpose.

- Block the essential:
  Protect time for your deepest work—your "sacred hours." Make these non-negotiable, defended as a fortress.
- Batch the shallow:
  Group errands, chores, correspondence. Confine the trivial to its own pen, lest it bleed into the wild.
- Rotate your obsessions:
  Let curiosity lead. When one field grows stale, pivot to another. Trust the seasons of fascination.
- Audit your attention:
  At week's end, reflect: Where did your mind wander? What did you feed it? What did you starve? Revise your dance accordingly.
- Celebrate incompletion:
  Let some projects remain unfinished, some questions remain open. The dance is not a march, but an endless festival.

IX. The Law of Chronomastery

Time is not your enemy, nor your servant. It is your partner in a lifelong dance. The polymath does not conquer time; she courts it, learns its rhythms, and lets her curiosity lead.

The world will try to schedule you into submission. Resist. Let your hours be wild, your attention sovereign, your dance unending.

Law of the Polymath #17:

Dance with time, do not march to its drum. Spend your attention as treasure, and let your life become a festival of worlds.

CHAPTER EIGHTEEN

THE SECRET CABINET — CULTIVATING HIDDEN ROOMS OF GENIUS

"Every mind is a palace, but only the curious build hidden rooms."
— From the lost journals of Athanasius Kircher

I. The Architecture of Hidden Genius

The world loves the visible: the résumé, the credentials, the public victories. We are taught to show our best rooms, to tidy the parlors of our minds for inspection. Yet all true genius flourishes in secrecy. The polymath knows that the greatest treasures are kept behind locked doors—unfinished, unshared, unspoiled by the gaze of others.

Cultivating hidden rooms is not deceit, but discipline. These are sanctuaries where the mind experiments, collects, obsesses, and plays without judgment or interruption. The secret cabinet is where the polymath rehearses her most audacious ideas, where half-born projects gestate, where heresy is safe from the torch of convention.

This is the paradox of brilliance: what is most original is often most private, most world-changing when least visible.

II. The Cabinet of Curiosities

In the Renaissance, scholars and nobles built Wunderkammern—cabinets of curiosity—filled with bones, coins, automata, and oddities. These were not collections for the public, but for the self: spaces of wonder, disorder, and private synthesis. The polymath's mind is a living Wunderkammer, a labyrinth of secret fascinations, hidden experiments, and forbidden thoughts.

The specialist displays his trophy case; the polymath builds a secret archive. Here lie:

- Unread books, annotated in the margins.
- Unfinished paintings, half-mad musical sketches.
- Mathematical puzzles, code fragments, diary confessions.
- Secret obsessions: the language of orchids, the logic of dreams, the history of vanished civilizations.

These are not distractions, but the roots of future revolutions. The secret cabinet is the laboratory where genius is distilled in darkness.

III. Parable: The Locked Study

A legend is told of a reclusive scholar who, for decades, never published a word. After his death, villagers broke into his study and found walls lined with manuscripts—equations, maps, poems, machines. At first, they despaired at the waste. But over generations, his secret work became a wellspring: scientists, artists, and inventors drew inspiration from his hidden rooms, building futures the scholar could never have foreseen.

The world's progress is seeded in the soil of private genius.

IV. The Rituals of Cultivation

How does the polymath tend her hidden rooms? Through deliberate, sacred practices:

1. **Private Journaling:**
   Keep notebooks no one will read. Write for your future self, for your ghosts, for the child within. Let these pages be wild, unfinished, unjudged.
2. **Secret Projects:**
   Maintain works-in-progress that are never shown. The secret novel, the silent symphony, the impossible invention. These are gardens where audacity can grow unpruned.
3. **Obsession as Incubation:**
   Follow your strangest curiosities in private. Allow yourself the luxury of becoming an expert in something useless, something beautiful, something forbidden.
4. **No Audience, No Applause:**
   Create without regard for reception. Genius is not a performance, but a process. The secret cabinet is the only space where the mind is wholly free.
5. **Periodic Pilgrimage:**
   Retreat to your hidden rooms at intervals. Let the world recede. Here, review your archives, revisit your failures, celebrate your oddities. Genius emerges in solitude and secrecy.

V. The Shadow Side: Hoarding and Hiding

Secrecy is a double-edged sword. Genius can wither in the dark, the mind can become a hoarder of its own riches. The risk is stagnation, paranoia, the paralysis of perfectionism. The secret cabinet must not become a tomb.

The art is balance: to cultivate privacy without fear, to cherish secrets without becoming enslaved to them. The greatest ideas will one day demand to see the light. The polymath must know when to open the cabinet, when to share, when to let her hidden rooms become corridors for other minds.

VI. The Secret Cabinet in History

History's greatest minds were architects of secrecy:

- **Isaac Newton** kept his alchemical research locked away, fearing ridicule and heresy.
- **Emily Dickinson** published only a handful of poems in her life, her genius revealed only after her death.
- **Ada Lovelace** filled her notebooks with visions of computers centuries ahead of their time—notes discovered long after her passing.
- **Nikola Tesla** died with trunks of unbuilt inventions, blueprints generations would later rediscover.

Their secret cabinets were not failures, but vaults for the future. The world is changed by what was once hidden.

VII. Parable: The Cabinet of Mirrors

In a distant city, a polymath constructed a cabinet of mirrors, each reflecting a different aspect of her mind—one for art, one for science, one for memory, one for desire. She closed the cabinet for years, fearing madness. Upon opening it again, she found that the mirrors had multiplied, reflecting new selves she had never consciously created. Her hidden rooms had become a universe.

VIII. The Polymath's Inner Sanctum

Every polymath requires a sanctum—a place, physical or mental, that is inviolable. Here, performance ceases. Here, the mind renews itself. The secret cabinet is the heart of perennial creativity, the wellspring that feeds the outward torrent of innovation.

The world will always hunger for your secrets, but you must guard some rooms for yourself alone. The greatest act of rebellion in an age of surveillance is to preserve the privacy of your genius.

IX. The Law of the Cabinet

True mastery is not paraded, but cultivated in silence. Genius is a garden best tended behind closed doors. The secret cabinet is not a retreat from the world, but the womb in which new worlds are conceived.

Let your mind be a palace of hidden rooms. Let your curiosity be the key.

Law of the Polymath #18:

Build secret cabinets within your mind. Let genius flourish in privacy, and bring forth your treasures when the world is ready to receive them.

CHAPTER 19: THE INSURGENT'S MANIFESTO — REWRITING THE LAWS OF LEARNING

"When the old laws imprison the mind, break them and write your own."
— Graffito, crumbling wall of a university, date unknown

I. The Tyranny of the Old Laws

From the moment of birth, you are bound by invisible decrees. The curriculum is scripted long before your first question; the path is signposted by unseen hands. "Learn in this order. Master this, then that. Do not wander. Do not doubt the canon." The world calls this education. The insurgent calls it indoctrination—an architecture of control, not of liberation.

The old laws of learning serve the needs of institutions, not individuals. They reward compliance, punish deviation, and prize the appearance of knowledge over its living flame. The specialist is their perfect subject: obedient, replaceable, blind to the worlds beyond his script.

The polymath, by inclination and necessity, is a natural outlaw. Her curiosity will not be fenced. Each forbidden question is a breach in the wall. Each secret obsession is a torch passed between rebels. When the world's laws of learning become shackles, the insurgent prepares to shatter them.

II. The Anatomy of Educational Control

The laws of learning are enforced by a priesthood of gatekeepers: teachers, testers, credentialers, committee-men. These are not always villains, but cogs in a system designed to preserve the status quo. Their commandments are clear:

- Knowledge is finite, and measured in credits.
- Questions are dangerous unless pre-approved.
- Failure is shameful, not instructive.
- Learning is a means to a job, not to freedom.
- The canon is closed. The experiment is over.

These laws breed timidity. The student learns not how to think, but how to pass. The mind, hungry for wildness, is tamed for the market.

But every era of stagnation breeds its heretics—those who refuse the curriculum, who teach themselves in the midnight hour, who write their own textbooks in the margins of the sanctioned page.

III. Parable: The School Without Walls

In a city where every street was a classroom, a group of children began to meet outside the school gates. They learned from the birds and the mechanics in the alley, from the bakers and the madmen and the clouds. They invented new games, new languages, new ways to count and sing. The teachers were horrified, the parents afraid. But in time, the city changed—its best inventions, its boldest art, its most dangerous questions all traced back to the school without walls.

The insurgent is always first a dropout, then a founder.

IV. The Manifesto of the Insurgent Learner

To rewrite the laws of learning is to declare independence from the curriculum of the crowd. The insurgent does not reject learning; she reclaims it, returning it to its primal force.

1. **Learn Obliquely:**
Go sideways. Seek the underground route, the forbidden shelf, the overlooked footnote. The insurgent's curriculum is not linear, but labyrinthine.

2. **Question Everything—Especially the Syllabus:**
Every prescribed order is a hypothesis, not a commandment. Dare to begin at the end, to invert the sequence, to write your own table of contents.

3. **Fail as a Ritual:**
Treat failure not as a mark of shame, but as the raw material of mastery. The insurgent fails often, fails creatively, fails forward.

4. **Build Your Own Guilds:**
Find co-conspirators. The best learning is a plot, a salon, a conspiracy. The insurgent's guild is not a closed circle but an open-ended dialogue of the curious.

5. **Teach to Learn:**
The best way to master is to teach what you do not yet fully know. The insurgent is always a teacher-in-training, always a student-in-action.

6. **Abandon the Fixed Point:**
Let your interests mutate. Begin as a scientist, become a musician,

end as a philosopher. The insurgent's mind is a river, not a canal.

V. The Insurgent's Curriculum

The new laws are not written in stone, but in sand—meant to be rewritten, revised, rebelled against:

- **Self-Directed Projects:**
  Build something real. Launch a journal, start a movement, code a tool, compose a song. The world is your laboratory.
- **Cross-Disciplinary Raids:**
  Raid other fields for ideas, metaphors, and methods. Bring them back to your own.
- **Learning by Play:**
  Gamify your study. Play with problems. Let curiosity, not fear, be your guide.
- **Public Experiments:**
  Share your process openly. Blog your failures, post your drafts, invite critique from unexpected quarters.
- **Lifelong Apprenticeship:**
  Find new mentors at every age. Learn from the young, the old, the outsider, the enemy.

The insurgent's education is never finished because the world is never finished.

VI. The Polymath as Revolutionary

Every revolution in knowledge has been led by insurgent polymaths:

- **Galileo** building telescopes in his workshop, defying the Church.

- **Mary Shelley** inventing science fiction at the margins of the literary world.
- **Alan Turing** crossing mathematics, cryptography, and logic to invent the modern mind.

The world remembers their triumphs, but forgets their rebellions—the years of exile, ridicule, poverty, and doubt. The insurgent pays a price for freedom. But the chains of consensus are heavier still.

VII. Parable: The Archive of Burning Books

A despot ordered every forbidden book in his city burned. The insurgents responded by memorizing the texts, reciting them in back alleys, scribbling them in code on walls, encoding them in song. The archive was not destroyed. It was scattered, multiplied, made immortal.

The insurgent's manifesto: what cannot be published must be lived.

VIII. The Rituals of Intellectual Insurgency

To become an insurgent in the world of learning:

- Break something every day:
  A rule, a habit, a paradigm.
- Ask heretical questions:
  Especially the ones that make others uncomfortable.
- Celebrate the unfinished:
  The insurgent's masterpiece is always a draft.
- Make learning visible:
  Let your process, not just your product, be your signature.
- Write new laws:

Every time you learn, ask: What would I forbid? What would I require? What would I invent?

IX. The Return of the Heretic

The world will not thank you for your insurgency. You will be ignored, mocked, or attacked. But you will be alive. Your mind will be your own. And in time, the world will follow where you have dared to break the trail.

Every new canon is written first in the margins, with stolen ink, by hands that refuse to be stilled. The insurgent's manifesto is not a text, but a way of being—a refusal to be learned, a determination to be learning.

X. The Law of the Insurgent

Learning is not obedience. It is rebellion. Write your own laws, burn the old, and teach the world by the firelight of your heresies.

Law of the Polymath #19:

Be the insurgent of your own education. Break the laws that bind your mind, and rewrite them in the ink of your restless curiosity.

CHAPTER TWENTY

THE LAST RENAISSANCE — AWAKENING THE POLYMATHIC REVOLUTION

"There is a dawn that comes not once, but whenever a single mind refuses to be divided."
— Fragment from the Testament of the Unfinished

I. The Long Night of Division

For centuries, the world has been shrinking. Not in its wonders, but in its vision. The map of human potential, once infinite and wild, has been redrawn into tight plots, each fenced and patrolled. The Renaissance—our last golden age—has become a myth, a painting hung in the museum of nostalgia, admired but never imitated. We are told the age of the polymath is over, that the world is too complex, too vast, too specialized for any one person to traverse its labyrinth.

But this is a lie of exhaustion, not of truth. The division of knowledge was an act of convenience, not necessity. The world did not outgrow the polymath; it banished her for threatening the order of the machine. The specialists built towers so tall they could no longer see the ground, or each other. We have gained power and lost vision. We have built engines and forgotten how to dream.

II. The Gathering Storm

Yet beneath the surface, a storm is gathering. The world's problems refuse the boundaries of the syllabus. Pandemics, climate change, artificial intelligence, social fracture—these are not issues of one field, but of many. The old order is breaking. The world is hungry for minds capable of synthesis, of vision, of crossing forbidden borders.

The internet, the great archive and agora, has revived the possibility of the polymath. The walls of the ivory tower are crumbling; the libraries are open all night; the guilds are dissolving. The tools of learning and creation—once hoarded by the few—are now scattered at the feet of the many. Still, abundance is not enough. The tools must be wielded by minds trained to leap, to question, to unite.

It is not enough to return to the Renaissance. The world demands something greater: a revolution of polymaths, a last Renaissance that will not be followed by another dark age.

III. Manifesto for the Polymathic Revolution

What does it mean to awaken the polymathic revolution?

1. Refuse Division:
   Reject the myth that you must choose between art and science, intuition and logic, play and rigor. The new age belongs to those

who build bridges, who speak in many tongues, who are unashamed to be many.

2. Make Curiosity a Practice of Defiance:

Let your learning be rebellion. Let every question be a spark. Refuse the curriculum, the credential, the boundary. Learn what the world forbids, and teach what the world has forgotten.

3. Synthesize Ruthlessly:

Do not wait for permission to connect, to cross-pollinate, to hybridize. The polymath's genius is in the leap, the analogy, the unthinkable alliance. Synthesis is your superpower.

4. Build New Guilds:

Find your kin among the misfits, the hackers, the heretics. The revolution will not be televised—it will be whispered in salons, in forums, in labs and garages, in code and ink and song.

5. Embrace the Unfinished:

The new Renaissance is not a return to old mastery, but a celebration of perpetual becoming. Do not mourn what you have not yet learned; hunger for what you might yet know.

6. Teach by Example:

Let your life be your argument. Become a living syllabus, a walking contradiction, a proof that it is possible to be many and whole.

IV. Parable: The City of Many Bridges

There once was a city divided by rivers. Each neighborhood built higher walls, mistrusting the others. The city grew rich in isolation, but poor in spirit. Then, during a terrible storm, the rivers rose and the walls crumbled. In the chaos, a few began to build bridges from the remnants. The city was remade not by its towers, but by its crossings. In time, the bridges became the city's pride, its lifeblood, its new way of being.

So too with the mind—its strength lies not in its partitions, but in its connections.

V. The Polymath's Oath

Let this be our oath, the creed of the Last Renaissance:

- I will not shrink to fit the world's compartments.
- I will feed all my hungers, and let no discipline starve.
- I will question every boundary, every canon, every law.
- I will seek the others—those who cross, who combine, who create.
- I will let my life be a bridge, and invite others to cross.

VI. The Dawn of the Last Renaissance

The polymathic revolution is not a movement of masses, but of individuals—each one a seed of the infinite. It is a revolution waged in quiet rooms and crowded forums, in ink and code and paint, in questions asked at midnight and dreams dreamt at dawn. It is not the work of a day, or an age, but the slow, relentless awakening of possibility.

The Last Renaissance is not a return, but a birth. It is the coming of the world that was always possible—the world of the whole mind, the undivided self, the living bridge.

VII. Law for the End and the Beginning

Let the last Renaissance begin with you. Let it never end.

Law of the Polymath #20:

Become the revolution. Refuse division. Build bridges. Let your life awaken the world's last, and greatest, Renaissance.

Afterword

"The end of one path is the beginning of a thousand more."
— From the Epistles of the Wanderers
You have walked with me through twenty chapters, across forbidden borders and into secret rooms, through solitude and synthesis, rebellion and ritual. But the true journey does not end here.

The world remains unfinished. The library is never complete. Each day brings new edges, new questions, new invitations to become more than you were yesterday. If this book has kindled even one spark—one act of curiosity, one bold question, one refusal to be reduced—then its work is done.

The age of the polymath is not a relic; it is a revolution waiting for your name. Carry these laws as tools, not as chains. Rewrite them as you grow. The last Renaissance is not behind us, but ahead, and it begins wherever you stand.

Thank you for daring the many.

Now go—multiply worlds.

About The Author

Rushan Khan is a restless wanderer in the worlds of code, language, and invention. With an All India Rank of 79 in IIT-JEE, he is pursuing Computer Science and Engineering at the Indian Institute of Technology Delhi. Rushan is a polyglot fluent in English, Hindi, French, German, Urdu, Arabic, Sanskrit, Russian, Cantonese, and Greek, and holds a Duolingo certification in multiple languages.His academic journey includes a physics diploma from Hansraj College (Delhi University), and seven research papers on ResearchGate. As a founder, he built Novasphere, a web development and fintech startup. His professional experience spans internships at Amazon India, NITI Aayog, DRDO India, ISRO, and the United Nations.Rushan is a full-time crypto and equity investor, a 3D graphics and Adobe software master, and an educator for children in need through the New Citizen Welfare Organisation. He shares his journey and polymathic insights with over 12,000 followers on Instagram (@iam.rushaan).This book is both a testament to and a toolkit for those who refuse to live as only one thing.

Further Reading & Resources

For those wishing to keep wandering, here is a non-exhaustive map of inspiration:

- Range by David Epstein
- How to Think Like Leonardo da Vinci by Michael J. Gelb
- Stealing Fire by Steven Kotler & Jamie Wheal
- The Medici Effect by Frans Johansson
- The Innovators by Walter Isaacson
- The Art of Learning by Josh Waitzkin
- Gödel, Escher, Bach by Douglas Hofstadter
- The Structure of Scientific Revolutions by Thomas S. Kuhn
- The Master and His Emissary by Iain McGilchrist
- Originals by Adam Grant
- Mindstorms by Seymour Papert
- Polymath communities, learning platforms, and cross-disciplinary journals

Online Resources:

- ResearchGate, JSTOR, arXiv
- Duolingo, Coursera, edX
- Indie hackers, Hacker News, and creative salons
- The @iam.rushaan Instagram community for dialogue and updates

Index

N

O

P

Q

R

W

Y

Z

KEY PEOPLE (index by chapter for cross-reference):

INDEX

Closing Invitation

"Every ending is a gate, every reader a bridge."
If you have reached this final page, know that you have not only completed a book—you have crossed a threshold. The true work, the real journey, begins now.
The world was not made for the many-minded.
You will be told, again and again, to return to the comfort of the single track, to trade your hunger for certainty, to let your wildness be tamed by the needs of the hour. The laws of the crowd will beckon you back—offering applause for obedience, safety for silence, belonging for the price of shrinking your dreams.
But you know now—because you have lived these pages—there is another way.
Let this book be your secret cabinet, your philosopher's stone, your map of the unthinkable. Let its laws guide you not as commandments, but as invitations: to rebel, to synthesize, to teach, to play, to build, to wander, to return, to begin again. You are not bound to be one thing. You are not condemned to a single room in the palace of your life.
The world aches for bridges—between disciplines, between cultures, between souls. You can be that bridge. In every meeting, in every project, in every question you ask, you carry the possibility of the next Renaissance. The polymathic revolution will not begin in parliaments or universities, but in the quiet refusal of a single mind to be divided.
If you feel alone on this path, remember: every true journey begins in solitude. But no journey worth taking is walked alone for long. Seek your kin—the heretics, the wanderers, the rebels who hunger for the infinite. Build new guilds, new schools, new sanctuaries for the many-minded. Become a teacher by example, a student by desire, a builder by compulsion.
And if, at times, you falter—if your curiosity burns low, if the world's noise grows too loud, if you doubt your own

multiplicity—return to these pages. They will remind you:
You are not a fragment. You are a constellation. You are the axis on
which the possible turns.
So, step beyond this final page.
Write your own law of the polymath.
Share your journey, inspire another, lift the torch higher.
Wherever you go, may you carry the fire of the many, and may you
ignite it in the hearts of all who wander with you.
The end of this book is not a closing, but a beginning.
The path ahead is yours to draw, and the world is waiting for the
bridges only you can build.
Meet me at the edge of the map.
There, we will begin again.
— Rushan Khan